STAYING SAFE AT SCHOOL

SECOND EDITION

STAYING SAFE
AT SCHOOL

SECOND EDITION

CHESTER L. QUARLES
TAMMY F. QUARLES

CRC Press
Taylor & Francis Group
Boca Raton   London   New York

CRC Press is an imprint of the
Taylor & Francis Group, an **informa** business

CRC Press
Taylor & Francis Group
6000 Broken Sound Parkway NW, Suite 300
Boca Raton, FL 33487-2742

© 2011 by Taylor and Francis Group, LLC
CRC Press is an imprint of Taylor & Francis Group, an Informa business

International Standard Book Number: 978-1-4398-5828-8 (Paperback)

Library of Congress Cataloging-in-Publication Data

Quarles, Chester L.
 Staying safe at school, second edition / Chester L. Quarles and Tammy Quarles.
 . -- 2nd ed.
   p. cm.
 Includes bibliographical references and index.
 ISBN 978-1-4398-5828-8 (pbk.)
 1. School violence--United States--Prevention. 2. Teachers--Crimes
against--United States--Prevention. 3. Schools--Security measures--United States. I.
Quarles, Tammy. II. Title.

LB3013.3.Q38 2011
371.7'820973--dc22   2010050666

Visit the Taylor & Francis Web site at
http://www.taylorandfrancis.com

and the CRC Press Web site at
http://www.crcpress.com

Contents

PREFACE   ix

ABOUT THE AUTHORS   xi

INTRODUCTION   xiii

CHAPTER 1   ARE YOU AFRAID?   1
            National Survey Shows Fear Level at School   2
            The Most Dangerous Place Is School   5
            You Can Make a Big Difference   7
            References   7

CHAPTER 2   CRIME PREVENTION   9
            Crime Prevention Can Be Accomplished by Almost Anyone 9
            Crime Reduction   10
            Four Elements of Crime   13
            Avoidance and Deterrence   15
            Victim Profile   16
            Four Stages of Crime   17
            References   19

CHAPTER 3   RISK ASSESSMENT   21
            Determine Your Risk Factor   21
            Making Risk Assessment Maps   22
            Hot Spots   23
            PINs   24
            Fear   26
            Receiving and Rating Information   26

A Reliability Index 28

References 29

CHAPTER 4 RISK REDUCTION 31

Put the U in Security 31

Risks Can Be Managed 32

Managing Your Risk 34

Join with Other Students 35

Are You a Target? 36

A Soft Target 36

A Hard Target 37

Friendliness 38

References 42

CHAPTER 5 YOUR PERSONAL SECURITY PROGRAM 43

Be Careful 44

Never Delegate Your Security 44

Personal Security 45

Be Alert 46

Be Friendly to All 47

Vigilance 47

Reference 48

CHAPTER 6 EVERYDAY SECURITY DECISIONS 49

Deciding on What to Wear 50

The Question of School Uniforms 50

Don't Let His Eye Stop on You 51

Knowing How to Walk 53

Deciding on What to Take with You and What to Leave
Behind 53

Street Crime Alarms 55

Learn to "Power" Yell 56

Communication Systems 56

Weapons or Pepper Spray 57

CHAPTER 7 TRAVELING SAFELY 59

Choose a Familiar Route 61

There Are Always Alternatives 62

Take Your Friends with You: Form Crime Avoidance
Partnerships 65

Using School and Public Restrooms 66

Bus or Subway Travel 68

Riding in a Taxi 69

If You Drive 70

Riding Your Bike 73

References 73

CHAPTER 8   AVOIDING TROUBLEMAKERS   75
Who Are the Troublemakers?   75
Bullies   76
Truants and Tardy Students   79
Weapon Carriers   79
Gang Members   80
Substance Abusers   84
Ritualistic Groups   85
Vigilantes   87
References   89

CHAPTER 9   BECOMING A SUCCESSFUL VICTIM   91
Winners and Losers   91
What to Do during a Robbery?   93
During a Gunfight   97
During a Fight   98
Bomb Scares   99
References   100

CHAPTER 10   TEENAGE RAPE AND SEXUAL ASSAULT
AVOIDANCE   101
Rape Can Happen to Anyone   102
Prerape Interviewing   104
Prerape Tests   104
Rape Myths   107
Date Rape Prevention   107
Date Rape   108
Watch the Men Watching You   111
References   112

CHAPTER 11   WHAT ARE YOU GOING TO DO NOW?   113
When You Are Attacked   113
Accept the Probability of Crime   114
Listen to Your Feelings   115
Accept the Responsibility   117
Being Prepared Has Tremendous Benefits   117
You Can Impact Crime   118
References   119

INDEX   121

Preface

Staying Safe at School focuses on the security approaches necessary for living and surviving in contemporary society. There isn't a fundamental difference between crime prevention and being a good citizen.

While you won't find profanity or vulgarity in these pages, you will find "straight" talk. While it is harmful to inappropriately label other teenagers, especially in a disparaging manner, we still must describe them properly. Defining individuals as *bullies, troublemakers, dopers, outlaws, crack heads, gangsters, creeps, thieves, prostitutes,* and *perverts* may not be politically correct, but it is quite functional. These terms are descriptive of varying forms of deviant behavior.

While we should ordinarily not be rude to these individuals, nevertheless, the average teenager does not necessarily have the experience, the maturity, or the wisdom to deal with these deviants.

There is another problem. Young girls are taught to be polite and lady-like. Boys are usually trained to be courteous in the average household. Herein lies the rub. Any form of aggression is frowned upon in the contemporary, middle-class household. We should recognize that there is no rule relating to "thou shalt not be rude." I am not suggesting that you be discourteous under normal circumstances, but, if people who give you the creeps are bothering you, you have permission to be discourteous.

Don't be afraid of fear, either. Look at fear like a guardian angel sitting on your shoulder—whispering, shouting, or even screaming the word *BEWARE*. As you read this book, you should become more aware of your surroundings and the people approaching or watching you. Don't be a Pollyanna. She was in denial 100 percent of the time. She thought that nothing bad would ever happen to her. Bad things do happen to good people, but they don't have to happen to you if you obey reasonable crime prevention rules. Learn these rules, practice these rules, live these rules, and you will be safer than you were without them.

About the Authors

Chester Quarles, PhD, is a professor emeritus of Criminal Justice and Homeland Security at the University of Mississippi, Oxford. During his career, he has served as a military policeman, a state policeman, as manager of the Mississippi Crime Laboratory, and later as the director of the Mississippi Bureau of Narcotics. He also is recognized as a "Certified Protection Professional" by the prestigious American Society for Industrial Security.

Much of his career has been spent studying crimes against children. As the father of five and the grandfather of 14, he is strongly motivated toward giving children and teens the skills they need to deal with bullies and criminals. This book is his fourth contribution to the field of school and community crime prevention for children and teenagers.

Tammy Quarles, M.Ed., is a Mississippi licensed professional counselor, a national board certified counselor, and a national certified school counselor. She has worked as a counselor for children ages prekindergarten through college. She also has served as a counselor in a variety of school settings, including an inner city, high crime, violent area. She is strongly motivated toward a safe work environment because she has worked in high-risk public schools and her daughter, Harlee, is currently a second grader at a local public school.

Quarles said when she entered teaching and, later, into the school counseling profession, that violence involving guns, knives, drugs, kidnapping, and rape were regrettably very frequent occurrences in the area surrounding her school. "We still had the tornado, fire, and earthquake drills, but now we had to add classroom lock down codes and response drills. We must combat crime at school and make schools safer for everyone. Administrators, teachers, counselors, staff, parents, and the community must work together and be persistent in the planning for and the prevention of future violence." She and her husband (a deputy U.S. Marshal), daughter, and son live in Oxford, Mississippi.

Introduction

Although schools often look like they are safe, appearances can be deceiving. Crime is frequent and there is more disruption than ever before. School is where young people and teenagers go to be disrespected, bullied, assaulted, robbed, and raped. Violence is a serious threat to education. Some schools have high crime rates because they are located in high crime areas, but many schools *are* the crime problem for the community.[1] Children are shot, stabbed, and murdered each day ... most often by other youth. ... In the United States about 15 youth under the age of 19 are murdered each day.[2] Almost 75 percent of youth murders are the result of gunfire.[3]

Recent studies indicate that more serious crimes are being committed at school. The age at which crimes are being committed is increasingly younger and the frequency of child and teen assaults is increasing.[4]

Eighty-three percent of all youth 12 years of age or older will become victims of actual or attempted violence during their lifetime, according to the U.S. Bureau of Justice Statistics.[5] There are many factors used in studying crime. One significant factor is *age*. Age is an element of victimization that you cannot control. You are either young, middle-aged, or older, but *the younger you are, the greater your risk.*

During one year prior to the Iraq War, 116 preschoolers died by gunfire in the United States—more than the number of police officers or of American soldiers killed in the line of duty during that same time span.[6]

The statistics are staggering. More American young people have been killed by guns in the past 13 years than were killed in Vietnam. Every year since 1950, the number of American children killed with guns has doubled. Every two days, 25 kids, the equivalent of an entire classroom, are murdered.[7]

Young children should be taught about crime and criminals as soon as they can comprehend this message. By the time a child leaves home for kindergarten, the child should have crime avoidance training. The purpose of the training is not to make the child distrustful, but to help the child avoid crime and criminals. Most parents discover that a child who develops crime avoidance habits at an early age will keep these habits throughout adolescence and on into adulthood. The youth needs to understand crime avoidance approaches, both in what they should do and what they must do to lower the chances that they will become a victim.

Recent School Shootings

August 17, 2010	Belleville, IL	1 dead
February 26, 2010	Tacoma, WA	1 dead
February 23, 2010	Jefferson County, CO	0 dead
February 6, 2010	Madison, AL	1 dead
September 16, 2009	Antioch, CA	0 dead
May 18, 2009	Larose, LA	1 dead
May 5, 2009	Canandaigua, NY	1 dead
November 12, 2008	Fort Lauderdale, FL	1 dead
October 16, 2008	Detroit, MI	1 dead
August 21, 2008	Knoxville, TN	1 dead
March 9, 2008	Mobile, AL	1 dead
February 12, 2008	Oxnard, CA	1 dead
February 11, 2008	Memphis, TN	0 dead
October 10, 2007	Cleveland, OH	1 dead
January 3, 2007	Tacoma, WA	1 dead
October 6, 2006	Nickel Mines, PA	6 dead
September 29, 2006	Cazenovia, WI	1 dead
September 27, 2006	Baily, CO	2 dead

August 30, 2006	Hillsboro, NC	1 dead	
August 24, 2006	Essex, VT	2 dead	
March 14, 2006	Reno, NV	0 dead	
December 6, 2005	Garden Grove, CA	1 dead	
November 17, 2005	Tampa, FL	1 dead	
November 8, 2005	Jacksboro, TN	1 dead	
November 5, 2005	Houston, TX	1 dead	
October 27, 2005	Fresno, CA	1 dead	
	San Leandro, CA	2 dead	
October 7, 2005	Richardson, TX	1 dead	
September 8, 2005	Richmond, CA	1 dead	
August 19, 2005	Miami, FL	1 dead	
March 21, 2005	Red Lake, MN	7 dead	
May 7, 2004	Randallstown, MD	0 dead	
April 3, 2004	Houston, TX	0 dead	
February 11, 2004	Philadelphia, PA	1 dead	
February 2, 2004	Washington, D.C.	1 dead	
January 13, 2004	Detroit, MI	0 dead	
November 14, 2003	East Mecklenburg, NC	0 dead	
October 30, 2003	Washington, D.C.	1 dead	
September 26, 2003	Cold Spring, MN	1 dead	
April 24, 2003	Red Lion, PA	2 dead	
April 14, 2003	New Orleans, LA	1 dead	
April 1, 2003	Washington, D.C.	0 dead	
December 16, 2002	Chicago, IL	1 dead	
December 12, 2002	Carson, WA	1 dead	
November 22, 2002	Dallas, TX	0 dead	
November 21, 2002	Chicago, IL	0 dead	
January 15, 2002	Manhattan, NY	0 dead	
November 13, 2001	Caro, MI	2 hostages	
April 3, 2001	Klein, TX	1 dead	
March 30, 2001	Gary, IN	1 dead	
March 22, 2001	El Cajon, CA	0 dead	
March 7, 2001	Williamsport, PA	0 dead	
March 5, 2001	Santee, CA	2 dead	13 injuries
February 3, 2001	Charleston, SC	1 dead	
February 2, 2001	Detroit, MI	0 dead	
January 17, 2001	Baltimore, MD	1 dead	
January 10, 2001	Oxnard, CA	1 dead	
December 7, 2000	San Pablo, CA	1 dead	
October 27, 2000	Memphis, TN	1 dead	
October 24, 2000	New York, NY	1 dead	

October 23, 2000	Los Angeles, CA	1 dead	
September 26, 2000	New Orleans, LA	0 dead	
September 13, 2000	Rock Island, IL	0 dead	
July 17, 2000	Renton, WA	0 dead	
May 26, 2000	Lake Worth, FL	1 dead	
March 23, 2000	Lisbon, OH	0 dead	
March 10, 2000	Savannah, GA	2 dead	
February 29, 2000	Mt. Morris Township, MI	1 dead	
December 6, 1999	Fort Gibson, OK	0 dead	
November 19, 1999	Deming, NM	1 dead	
May 20, 1999	Conyers, GA	0 dead	6 injuries
April 20, 1999	Littleton, CO	15 dead	20 injuries
April 16, 1999	Notus, ID	0 dead	
June 15, 1998	Richmond, VA	0 dead	
May 21, 1998	Springfield, OR	2 dead	22 injuries
May 21, 1998	St. Charles, MO	Police prevented this attack	
May 21, 1998	Onalaska, WA	1 suicide	
May 21, 1998	Houston, TX	0 dead	
May 19, 1998	Fayetteville, TN	1 dead	
April 28, 1998	Pomona, CA	2 dead	
April 24, 1998	Edinburo, PA	1 dead	
March 24, 1998	Jonesburo, AR	5 dead	10 injuries
December 1, 1997	West Paducah, KY	3 dead	5 injuries
October 1, 1997	Pearl, MS	2 dead	7 injuries
February 19, 1997	Bethel, AK	2 dead	
January 27, 1997	West Palm Beach, FL	1 dead	
February 2, 1996	Moses Lake, WA	3 dead	
January 18, 1993	Grayson, KY	1 dead	
May 1, 1992	Olivehurst, CA	4 dead	10 injuries
January 17, 1989	Stockton, CA	5 dead	30 injuries
September 26, 1988	Greenwood, SC	2 dead	9 injuries
May 20, 1988	Winnetka, IL	2 dead	
January 21, 1985	Goddard, KS	1 dead	
January 29, 1979	San Diego, CA	2 dead	7 injuries

During this time period, there were many additional injuries. (*Note*: Injuries less than five per event were not recorded in the statistical data referenced here.) School violence is now a worldwide phenomenon. During this same time period, school shootings were reported in Argentina, Azerbajan, Bosnia, Canada, Finland, Germany, Greece, Hungary, India, Israel, Lebanon, Norway, the Philippines, Scotland,

Sweden, Thailand, and the United Kingdom. Additionally, there were numerous shooting events at community colleges, technical schools, colleges, and universities.

Americans are at the greatest risk of becoming crime victims during their teenage years. In 2002, almost one in every four violent crimes involved a victim aged 12 to 17.[8] Teenagers are more than twice as likely to be victims of violent crime than those over the age of 20.[9]

Change the Circumstances of Your Crime

Staying Safe at School can help you learn about crime and violence avoidance. It will show you how to perform a "risk assessment" to determine if you should feel threatened. Some teenagers are unnecessarily frightened. Others are blissfully unaware of the incredible danger facing them each day. This book also will show you how to lower your risk and increase your safety. It will show you how to recognize the troublemakers and to prevent trouble. It will show you what to do in a crisis, and more importantly, what *not* to do. If your crime avoidance plan fails and you become a victim, the book also will show you approaches that will improve your chances of survival.

In many crimes, risks can be reduced to almost nothing because of changes in the lifestyles of potential victims. If you will follow the strategies recommended in this book, your chances of being victimized by predators will be considerably reduced, both at school and in the community.

There are very few random crimes. Most are planned. You can't stop the plan, but *you can change the circumstances*. You can force criminals and bullies to alter their plans. You can alter the likelihood of "your" assault. You can get "your" perpetrator (perp) to plan an attack against someone else. A teenager who avoids the more dangerous areas of the school and the community, who walks with friends, who develops crime avoidance partnerships, who is friendly to all, and who avoids conflict whenever possible is less likely to be attacked. Staying in public view deters virtually every type of crime. All attacks can't be stopped, but any action that increases the difficulty of an assault or that decreases the likelihood of the criminal getting away is effective.

Facing Your Fear

This is also a book about facing fear. It is a book about moral, physical, and spiritual courage. Courage is not the absence of fear; it is the control of fear.[10] Fear is a weapon you can use if you can control it, but it can be used by your enemies if you do not.[11] This book is *not* about fighting, karate, judo, physical defense, mace, pepper spray, or the use of weapons. In truth, your safety level *goes down* when anyone takes a weapon to school, but, if you do what this book says, *you will be safer.* This book shows you how to work with other students, teachers, counselors, and administrators to increase the safety of all. By applying what you will learn from this book, you can avoid criminal attack while protecting yourself and assisting others, as they avoid crime.

In your home, school, and community, you will be safest when you are centered in and are focused on being a good student, making good grades, and obeying school policies and rules. These standards and these values are also trouble-avoiding mechanisms. Sometimes, however, a teenager is threatened because of a value standard. The threat may occur when the biggest, meanest, and most abusive bully at your school insists that you write his homework assignment today. While you may not object to helping him, you also know that it is unethical to let him turn in your work as if it is his. So you have a problem. And, if your bully is really big and mean, you have a BIG problem. *Staying Safe at School* will show you how to deal with your bully.

Our hope is that you will learn how to prevent, deter, and avoid crime, but also that you will grow in knowledge both of crime threats and the necessary responses required. It is our desire that you accept the challenges of a crime prevention lifestyle.

Chester L. Quarles
Tammy Quarles

References

1. Jackson, T. 1983. Crime in the schools. In *Crime and public policy*, ed. J. Q. Wilson, 70. San Francisco: Institute for Contemporary Studies.
2. Fike, R. A., Sr. 1994. *Staying alive: Your crime prevention guide*. Washington D.C.: Acropolis Books Ltd., 16.
3. Ibid., 17.
4. Stevens, R. 1995. *Safe schools: A handbook for violence prevention*. Bloomington, IN: National Education Service, 13.
5. Brewer, J. D. 1994. *The danger from strangers*. New York: Insight Books, Plenum Press, 31.
6. Press release. 1996. Children's Defense Fund. April 9, 2.
7. Day, N. 1996. *Violence in schools: Learning in fear*. Springfield, NJ: Enslow Publishers, 32.
8. Sautter, R. C. 1995. Standing up to violence, *Phi Delta Kappan* January, k1–k2.
9. Ibid.
10. Brewer, *Danger from strangers*, 11.
11. L'Amour, L. 1984. *The proving trail*. New York: Bantam Doubleday Dell, 109.

1

ARE YOU AFRAID?

Jimbo Lane and his sister, Katie, saw a local teenage tough attack a 10-year-old kid right after school. Billy really hurt the little boy. They reported the incident and gave the principal the bully's name. Somehow Billy figured out who told on him and now he is harassing the Lanes. A big, rough fellow, he shoved Jimbo down a flight of stairs and he touched Katie's breasts, making coarse sexual remarks. He says that he has just "begun to get even with them for 'messing' with him." The intensity of Billy's attacks on Jimbo and Katie is rapidly escalating.

Jimbo and Katie are frightened and don't know what to do. They are keeping this problem a secret as well. Their mom, a single parent, already has a lot of problems and they don't want her to be worried about their safety too. But, if the assaults get any worse, Jimbo will be visiting the hospital emergency room. If the assaults intensify against Katie, she will be raped. She's already been groped, but, so far, her attacks were not witnessed.

Katie hasn't told Jimbo about Billy touching her breasts because she is afraid that Jimbo will fight Billy. Jimbo's a lot smaller, so he will most certainly lose any fight with the bully. So far, Katie just said that Billy was harassing her and she is scared. They both are afraid. What should they do? What should they *not* do? They have decided to discuss their options with the school counselor.

The counselor advised them to tell everything to their mother, even the sexual touching part, which was very embarrassing for Katie. The Lane family made an after-school appointment, and the mother, Katie, and Jimbo met with the students' counselor and principal. Billy has been a real trouble-maker for quite some time, but there were very few complaints from students against him, probably because they were afraid. This time, however, he had gone too far. He was already on in-school probation and that hadn't worked, so the principal decided to transfer Billy to an alternative school where his behavior could be more closely supervised. The principal thanked the Lane family for coming forward with the information he needed to document the bullying behavior. Billy would not even be told of these specific complaints. He would just be told that he has misbehaved and bullied little kids too often to remain.

National Survey Shows Fear Level at School

One recent national survey of middle and high school students conducted by the National School Safety Center discovered that over 800,000 young people stay home at least once a month because they are *afraid* to go to school.[1] This figure includes about 8 percent of the entire school population.[2] They don't play hooky to watch a soap opera or to go fishing. They stay home because they want to keep their dignity, their Nikes, the same clothes they went to school in, their homework, and their lunch money. They just don't want to be *dissed* (disrespected), so they stay home from school.

Fear is the primary concern of all students, according to one recent national study.[3] Because 89 percent of all school crime is committed by other students,[4] many students are afraid to go to school.[5] Serious crimes against kids usually occur on school property. One national survey showed that the risk of robbery is greater in school than outside of school;[6] another showed that 7 percent of all the violent acts committed at school involved the crime of rape.[7]

American schools have a high drop-out rate, with many kids never graduating from high school. Being afraid is one of the reasons kids drop out and this fear is totally unrelated to academics. Fear of other students is the reason 1 out of every 12 students reports dropping out of school,[8] according to one study. These students are literally "pushed out" of school—by violence, intimidation, and fear. They didn't *drop* out, they were *pushed* out.[9] Chances are that you have been afraid or you wouldn't have picked up this book, so perhaps you understand their fear.

If the title of this book attracted your attention, then you are afraid or, at least, concerned about your safety at school, at home, and in your community. Maybe you are scared to death; some teenagers even get sick to their stomach because they are so frightened. Others are so tense, they shake.

This book is about "people fear," where strangers, older students, gang members, bullies, or drug pushers frighten you. This book is about fear of fists, gangs, drugs, knives, and guns. Five out of six of today's 12-year-old children will be the subject of violence as serious as felony assaults, robber, rape, or murder.[10] During their lifetime, half of these children will face violence twice by the age of 12.[11] Homicide is the leading cause of death among African-American males aged 15 to 19 and the second leading cause of death for all youth.[12] The Children's Defense Fund projected that an American child is 15 times more likely to be killed by gunfire than a child living in Northern Ireland,[13] where Irish Republican Army and revolutionary Catholic violence had been a daily occurrence before a recent cease-fire peace agreement.

Many parents believe that gun-wielding, violence-prone students are a product of the past few years, but this is incorrect. Nationwide, between September 1986 and June 1990, at least 75 people were killed with guns at school, over 200 were wounded, and at least 243 were held hostage at schools by gun-wielding assailants.[14] The carnage continued into the late 1990s as Eric David Harris and Dylan Klebold murdered 12 students and a teacher and injured 23, in a "spree" killing before committing suicide. In 2005, seven were killed at a school in Red Lake, Minnesota. In 2006, six were killed at school in Nickel Mines, Pennsylvania.

It is not just the "spree" killer students who are taking guns to school. Spree killers shoot indiscriminately, although some of their victims are carefully selected. These victims are shot first and the shooters kill until they are either satisfied with their violence, run out of bullets, are arrested, or are killed by the police. The Children's Defense Fund studied this problem in 1991 and estimated that 135,000 children bring guns to school every day.[15] A more conservative study in 1993 by the largest American teachers association predicted that 100,000 children carry guns to school.[16] The word *children* is used because some kindergartners, first graders, and those in other grade-levels of elementary schools are bringing guns to school as well.

Even if you aren't afraid for yourself, maybe you are afraid for your little brother or sister. Are you afraid for a friend who is weaker or less assertive than you or are you concerned about the safety of your boyfriend or girlfriend? Test your fear level. The truth is that fear levels are increasing; more middle and high school students are afraid. Interestingly enough, junior high (middle school) is more dangerous than lower or higher grade levels.[17] Private interviews and questionnaires clearly demonstrate that the teenager fear level is higher than it was three years ago.

Males between the ages of 15 and 17 commit most juvenile crimes and the delinquent behavior decreases after age 17.[18] Victims can't control the age factor. You can't grow any faster and the younger you are the greater your risk. Younger persons and teens are at a risk that is nearly eight times higher than the risk for older adults.[19]

Students are often afraid to go to school. Sometimes you tell your parents about your fear, but it is likely your parents don't relate to your situation. When they grew up, gangs were relatively harmless, just groups of kids "goofing off" and maybe getting into occasional trouble. Every school had a bully.

Assault weapons were less sophisticated and more difficult to obtain during your parents' youth. Today, assault weapons are often purchased *at* school. In many cases, the school *is* the neighborhood weapon store. Count all the guns and knives at your school. You may determine that an arsenal is already there. Maybe this book will help you to "open up" and discuss the safety and security issues that you face at school and in your community. Talk (communicate) with your parents, to your counselor, and to police officials about these issues. Let them know how you feel and what you are seeing.

CONSIDER THESE FACTS

- Juveniles commit nearly one third of all serious crime in the United States (FBI, Uniform Crime Report).
- The school-age population includes the primary criminals in the United States. Nearly 50 percent of all police arrests involve the school-age population (National Institute of Education).

- In the average street crime, kids are eight times more at risk than adults. The younger you are, the more your risk (*Danger from Strangers*, 39).
- Murder by firearms is the number one cause of death for African-American males and the second leading cause of death for all young American males (Center to Prevent Handgun Violence in America).
- If you are in the age range from 10 to 20, you are 15 times more likely to be murdered than your parents (*School Safety* 101).
- Over 40 percent of all crimes against young people occur at school (The National School Safety Center).
- No one, regardless of age, race, sex, or economic status, is free from the threat of physical assault (Brewer, 6).

The Most Dangerous Place Is School

Your parents often do not understand that your school is the most dangerous place you go. Usually parents are concerned most about the mall, the movie theater, the bowling alley, or the youth game rooms. Statistical studies show that their concerns are appropriate, but perhaps misplaced. The fact is that you are more likely to become a crime victim *at school* than anywhere else[20] and about 8 percent of the nation's schools have a serious crime problem.[21]

The most dangerous time to be in school is the junior high or middle school years. This is almost universal, all across America. Assaults and robberies are twice as great in junior high as in senior high school.[22] Freshman and sophomore students commit more crimes at school than those in other grade levels.[23] Approximately 282,000 students are physically attacked in America's secondary schools each month.[24] Including these attacks, there are nearly 500,000 shakedowns, robberies, and attacks each month.[25]

The figures, however, don't show the complete problem. School crime affects more than just the victim and the school criminal. It affects the entire school, the educational atmosphere, and the morale of all who attend. Teenagers become distrustful, fearful, angry, frustrated, and increasingly rebellious in a dangerous environment.

According to the National Center for Education statistics, many of our public schools are "no longer safe places of learning."[26] According to the National School Safety Center, at least 40 percent of all crimes against children and teenagers occur at school.[27] Because you spend only about 25 percent of your total "waking hours" at school, the school crime rate is disproportionate in terms of other crime in your community. There is a strong truth in crime statistics, however. This truth is that, for a young person, the most dangerous place is school, so be prepared, be alert, and be ready to respond to threats of violence.

> The most dangerous place for a young person is school (National School Safety Center).
> Risk of assault and robbery to urban youngsters aged 12–19 is greater in school than at any other location (Vestermark and Blauvelt).

Parents often give advice based on their own experiences. In discussing a bully, many fathers will tell a teenage son, "If you fight back, he will pick on someone else." Your parents' experiences were quite different, however, than the scenarios you face every day. In their youth, students usually fought with their fists. The end result was a skinned knuckle, a black eye, or a sore mouth. Usually, the worst injury was an altered dentistry.

Today, however, many school-age criminals and gang members bring guns and knives to school. The *U.S. News and World Report Magazine* reported in April 6, 1998, that approximately 20 percent of all high school students *regularly* carry a firearm, knife, razor, or club to school. While this is probably an overstatement, there is no doubt that many students bring weapons to school. Today's fights end with broken bones, slashed arteries, stab wounds, bullet holes, paralysis, and death. Fighting should always be the last option on your list of alternatives.

You Can Make a Big Difference

You can make a difference at your school and in your community. You can be a leader in promoting safety and security. You can influence your school, your neighborhood, and your home. First of all, remember that you are not alone and you are not without resources. You are not powerless. You have a lot of personal influence, if you will just step in, step up, and speak out. The safest schools in America are the best schools, offering the best training and teaching. Students in safe schools succeed in English, mathematics, and the sciences, instead of the three "disruption Rs"—rape, robbery, and rebellion ... or reading, *riting*, and razor blades. Schools with good teachers have a good learning ratio. Their students score well on national examinations and college entrance test scores. Kids who have a desire to go to college can continue their education after attending "safe" schools.

Good students and good teachers enjoy safer schools. You, personally, make a difference in safety when you do your best in each of your classes, when you avoid clowning around or causing other disruptions, and when you obey the reasonable requirements set forth at your school.

References

1. Hill, M. S., and F. W. Hill. 1994. *Creating safe schools: What principles can do.* Thousand Oaks, CA.: Sage Publications, 43.
2. National School Safety Center. 1993. *Educated public relations, School safety 101.* Oak Park, CA: NSSC.
3. Greenbaum, S., B. Turner, and R. D. Stephens. 1989. *Set straight on bullies.* Oak Park, CA: The National School Safety Center, 9.
4. Fike, R. A., Sr. 1994. *Staying alive: Your crime prevention guide.* Washington, D.C.: Acropolis Books, 100.
5. Greenbaum et al. *Set straight on bullies*, 9.
6. National Institute of Education. 1978. *Violent schools—safe schools: The safe school study report to Congress.* Washington, D.C.: Government Printing Office, 13.
7. Day, N. 1996. *Violence in schools: Learning in fear.* Springfield, NJ: Enslow Publishers, 58.
8. Greenbaum et al. *Set straight on bullies*, 9.
9. Goldstein, A. P., and C. R. Huff, eds., 1993. *The gang intervention handbook.* Champaign, IL: Research Press, 269.

10. Powers, T. and R. B. Isaacs. 1993. *The seven steps to personal safety.* New York: Center for Personal Defense Studies, 5.

11. Ibid.

12. Lawton, M. 1992. Public health crisis: Teenage gun violence. *Education Week,* June 17, 14.

13. Children's Defense Fund. 1994. *The state of America's children: 1994.* Washington, D.C.: Children's Defense Fund.

14. Gaustad, J. 1991. Schools respond to gangs and violence. *Oregon School Study Council Bulletin* 34 (9).

15. Children's Defense Fund. 1991. *The state of America's children.* Washington D.C.: Children's Defense Fund, 42.

16. *Annual report to membership.* 1993. Washington, D.C.: National Education Association, 13.

17. Toby, J. 1983. *Violence in school.* A U.S. Department of Justice Monograph from the National Criminal Justice Reference Service, 29.

18. National School Boards Association. 1984. *Toward better and safer schools: A school leader's guide to delinquency prevention.* Washington, D.C.: Department of Justice, grant no. 82-MU-AX-K045.

19. Brewer, J. D. 1994. *The danger from strangers.* New York: Plenum Press, 39–40.

20. Vestermark, S. D., and P. D. Blauvelt. 1978. *Controlling crime in the school: A complete security handbook for administrators.* West Nyack, NY: Parker, 33.

21. Asher, M. R., and J. Broschart. 1978. Violent schools–safe schools: The safe school study report to the Congress. In *Topical bibliography on violence and vandalism in schools* (p. 156). Washington, D.C.: Juvenile Justice Clearing House, Department of Justice.

22. Toby, *Violence in School.*

23. Berra, P. M. 1978. Study of high school students in five offense categories. (unpublished) PhD diss., Arizona State University. In *Topical bibliography on violence and vandalism in schools,* 70. Washington, D.C.: Juvenile Justice Clearing House, Department of Justice.

24. National School Safety Center, *Educator Public Relations.*

25. Ibid.

26. The National Center for Education Statistics. 1998. *Violence and discipline problems in public schools: 1996–1997, Exec. Summ.* Washington, D.C.: Department of Education, February, 2–4.

27. Regnery, A. F. 1984. Report of Narrative Statement to the U.S. Senate Subcommittee on Juvenile Justice. Washington, D.C.: Administrator of the Office of Juvenile Justice and Delinquency Prevention, January 25, 2–3.

2

CRIME PREVENTION

Bobby is concerned about crime at his school. He has seen several criminal assaults and some of the victims left school in an ambulance. He's even seen girls abused. Bobby is a big, strong fellow himself, so the bullies and the gangsters pretty much leave him alone. He is really concerned about some of his friends, however, and also about his little brother, Billy. What can Bobby do to help? One thing he can do is to get together with other students and the faculty to help decrease the violence. Just as he is aware of the crimes at school, others must learn of it, too. Talking to your parents, to school counselors, or trusted teachers about this issue is a good start. By working with the truth, which is that students are not safe at this school, the students and faculty can work together to successfully reduce the violence, substance abuse, and crime levels in the school while increasing the academic standards. This chapter will show you how.

Remember, school counselors can play a vital role in the early detection and possibly the prevention of school violence. It is their job to deal with disruptive students of all types and to help prevent school violence. They have a legal and ethical duty, as well as the responsibility, to take action and prevent the possible harm of others and also to the welfare of the potential violent student. The Supreme Court, in *Davis v. Monroe County Board of Education* (1999), documented that school personnel are on notice to protect students and that they may be held personally responsible for failing in that duty.[1]

Crime Prevention Can Be Accomplished by Almost Anyone

Crime prevention can be very simple. It is any approach that protects the potential victim from harm. The first requirement is that a potential victim must be *alert*. The second requirement is that the potential victim also must be *aware*. By being aware of a threat or by anticipating a possible attack, the potential victim reduces or even eliminates a crime opportunity.

Crime prevention strategy is like a road map. If you want to travel from one city to an unknown location, you will need a map. The map shows you the best routes. So it is with a risk avoidance strategy or a security plan. By following a plan, you are safer than the individual who doesn't have one.

Crime Reduction

There are certain ingredients necessary for a crime. It's like a recipe. If any of the crime ingredients are missing, there is no crime. Influencing these "ingredients" lowers your risk.

CRIME INGREDIENTS

- Desire on the part of the criminal
- Skill on the part of the criminal
- Opportunity to commit the crime

There is very little you can do about criminal desire. Some kids are thieves, just as are some adults. They want what others have, even if they already have enough. While you can't change their minds, their ethics, or their desire, you can dress in ways that minimize their desire to steal the things you have. A $20 pair of tennis shoes is much less desirable than a $300 pair of Nikes. A reasonable quality value store jacket purchased for $28 will keep you warm in the winter, but it is much less likely to be coveted than a $385 wool and leather NFL jacket. It is highly improbable that the thief would try to steal the $20 tennis shoes or the $28 jacket. Dressing inexpensively can prevent you from being the victim of a robbery. It can even save your life

> Dressing inexpensively can save your life.

because you avoided the very robbery that could end up resulting in your being killed.

Likewise, it is difficult to undermine a criminal's skill. He is either an experienced crook or he isn't. He learns by doing. Either he has a lot of experience at crime or he has little, or none. Even if he is experienced, you can lower your risk by increasing his. This can be accomplished by using the buddy system or by traveling in groups with other teenagers. The toughest bully or thief is not likely to challenge the group. He would prefer to catch one teenager alone and to isolate him or her out of public view.

Opportunity is the last area of influence. You decrease the criminal's opportunity when you dress in less expensive clothes and when you travel in a group. You decrease criminal opportunity when you take a safer route through your neighborhood. At night, you reduce opportunity by staying near the edge of the sidewalk and walking under the streetlights rather than taking shortcuts through dark alleys.

UNDERSTAND HOW CRIMINALS OPERATE

By understanding *how* criminals operate in your town and knowing *where* they operate and *at what time* they operate, you can reduce your risk opportunity.

Our national government's response to skyjacking is a formidable example of opportunity reduction. Back in the 1970s, revolutionaries frequently skyjacked airplanes filled with passengers. It happened all the time, but you rarely hear much about skyjacking today. Why? Skyjacking is rare today because of *opportunity reduction*. Sky marshals, security checkpoints, metal detectors, and bomb detecting dogs have lowered the risk considerably. Revolutionaries don't skyjack as much because we have reduced their opportunity to do so successfully. This can be applied to other offenses, as well. The number of crimes will be reduced as criminal opportunity is lowered.

You also should develop a good eye for deception. Certainly you don't want to create a world of safety in your mind, one that doesn't exist in reality. Realize that there is good in the world, but that crime co-exists with the good. Read the newspaper headlines. Read the crime section of your newspaper. Look at the nightly news on television or listen to a radio newscast daily.

See the world as it is, not the world you would prefer it to be. Danger is all around us, but most American teenagers fail to see it until it is too late. Often, middle-class teenagers are naïve and trusting. We believe that our institutions are safe, but often our safety is not real—it is a product of imaging. The safety isn't real, it exists only in our mind.

Never be lulled into security complacency. Just because nothing bad has happened over the past week or two doesn't mean that a crime is not about to occur *right now*. If you want to survive, you not only must play the criminals' game, you must play it better than he/she does.

If someone gives you the creeps or if you feel the hair on the back of your neck standing up, avoid that person. If you get the creeps at a particular location, do your best to avoid that site. *Listen to your feelings*. Watch, look, and listen. Don't let anyone else talk you out of those feelings. Don't talk yourself out of these feelings, either.

Often, when something is wrong, you get a feeling about it. We call this "listening to your gut." It's an important warning signal. Many times our instincts know we're in danger before our minds do. When you get a bad feeling about a place or a person, don't ignore it. Leave the place, get away from that person, do whatever you have to do to be safe.[2]

CRIME OPPORTUNITY MODEL

- A motivated offender
- A suitable target
- The absence of guardians

The crime opportunity model indicates that your risk increases when you are exposed to criminals. Your risk continues to increase in the absence of capable guardians. Most young people have never been victimized before they attended school. Why? The reason is that their mom, dad, or an older family member was usually with them when they were younger. It is only when they start school, *and are truly alone at their bus stop,* that there is no one, no adult, no guardian, to intervene in their behalf.

FOUR ELEMENTS TO EVERY CRIME

1. The act itself. A crime is an act made punishable by law.
2. The criminal or the violator. It is hard to deal with the criminal once the crime is in motion.
3. The victim. You can learn to avoid crime and avoid behavior that increases your chances of victimization.
4. The place. This is where you can change things because you control or at least influence your space.

Four Elements of Crime

Some criminologists focus on the elements of the crime as well as other related issues. Some claim that there are four elements inherent in every crime rather than just three. First, there must be a law violation. It is against the law to steal, to burn a building, to harm someone else, or to kill. For an event to be a crime, it must be against the law, recorded in your state, county, or city statute book. Some laws relate to issues that are evil (*mala en se)* like murder and arson or rape. Some laws refer to offenses, such as paying taxes, drug laws, speeding, or running stop signs (*mala prohibita).*

The law is hard to influence. If you want to get a law passed about school crime, drug trafficking, or gang violence, you must ask your local legislators or city councilpersons to initiate legislation. Sometimes laws are passed very quickly. The U.S. Anti-Terrorism Bill sailed through Congress after the Oklahoma City bombing attack. The Patriot Act, another controversial law, was passed shortly after 9/11. However, it usually takes many years before a legislative body changes the existing law or codifies a new law.

The second element of every crime is the victim. A robber takes money from his or her victim. The arsonist burns down a building owned by an individual, a corporation, or a governmental unit. If someone steals your car or robs you at gunpoint, then you are the victim. The victim can do a lot of things to influence his or her risk, so you will need to work hard to prevent a crime from happening to you.

LOWER YOUR RISK

You can lower your chances considerably that you will ever be a crime victim. You must know, however, that it is your responsibility to prevent a crime from happening to you.

The third element of every offense is the criminal. Law enforcement officers call the crook a *perpetrator* or use the abbreviated term *perp*. It is hard to influence a perp (this is a good name for a sorry, contemptible thief or a bully). Thieves steal because they don't have to pay for goods or services when they steal. However, we can build in crime barriers to make it harder for criminals to commit crimes.

The fourth element of every crime is place. The place can be crime free or it can be a nightmare. Schools can lower the risk factors. Your school can influence criminals by locking all but the front door during school hours. This creates a choke point for all visitors and intruders. Some call this activity *access control*. Access control is just one form of environmental crime prevention. Everyone must gain entrance through this door. Usually the guest entrance is adjacent to the principal's office. Visitor badges are obtained here. Intruders or those who do not have legitimate business at the school are turned away.

Most schools enjoy some form of environmental crime control. The long hallways are open and easily observed. Many schools have intersecting hallways, so a teacher or staff member can supervise the activities of students in four directions by standing at a hallway intersection. This increases the safety and security of all students.

Schools also can install video cameras. The student criminal is made to believe that his crime will be video recorded. If he believes that it is likely he will be identified, that he will be arrested later, or that he will not be able to escape the property without risking police capture, he will likely go somewhere else. School authorities and students can make a difference when they apply environmental crime prevention approaches. Working together, one can create an environment where the criminal feels out of place, insecure, and out of control. You can create a place where he feels he will be seen, identified, and arrested.

The treatment of the location by school authorities, security personnel, and the police department is called environmental security (ES). When a school is planned around ES principles, the approach is usually called CPTED (Crime Prevention through Environmental Design). There is no doubt that some locations are environmentally designed to decrease crime. This is the way that your school should be constructed, with an openness and clear visibility that in itself deters crime. If a new school is being designed by an architect, get your parents to insist on good surveillability and other environmental security benefits. Ask your English teacher or counselor to help you write a letter to the school board based on your fears and your safety concerns.

Avoidance and Deterrence

If you understand how crimes occur and how criminals operate, you will become more aware of local criminal activity. You will see when a crime is unfolding in front of you. Understanding the elements of crime (the criminal, the victim, and the place) can help you plan a successful avoidance and deterrence program.

There are several options. First, you may choose to report school crime, even if you do it anonymously by telling the principal, your counselor, or a trusted teacher. You also can influence your student government. Go into campus politics, run for office yourself. Even if you don't actively participate in student politics, you can ask your student council to establish rules against weapons, drugs, and gangs.

The principal already enforces some of these rules, which are probably published in your *Student Handbook*, but sometimes student rules and a student-approved Code of Conduct are much more important than the policies administered by adults. So, take some responsibility and make the decision to take charge and make a difference.

Students working together can make a lot of difference. Talk to your principal about security problems at your school. Start a Student Crime Watch Program. Recruit some of the best students out of study hall, pair them up, and let them be hall monitors or serve on a student security patrol. Fellow students can help lower the crime threat at your school.

Maybe your mom and dad are a part of your local Neighborhood Watch program. This is a good plan and you can use a similar one at your school. Some schools have parent or grandparent volunteer security patrols. If your dad or mom gets off work at the right time, he or she may be able to volunteer for patrols either immediately before, during, or after school, together or separately. Sometimes, just the presence of another adult will make all of the difference in the world. These adult or peer *guardians* do make a difference. They decrease disruption and crime and they increase safety and security.

Cooperate with your teachers, counselors, and administrators to create a safer school. Maybe you would like to help design a crime prevention program unique to

> Start a Student Watch Program or a Student Justice and Mediation System.

your school. Start a student justice system with the approval of school administrators and publish the new rules. Make sure that everyone is properly informed of the new rules and give at least a week's notice before implementing them. Usually parents receive a mail-out or you will be asked to hand-carry the notification as well.

Student justice systems help settle disagreements, which avoids confrontations and violence. Just be sure you are consistent and that the rules that students agree to are uniformly applied.

Victim Profile

All of us know people who are accident prone. Thelma Jones has already had three fender benders, and she is only 16 years old. Bobby Addy is always getting hurt doing something idiotic. Last year he broke his front teeth on a telephone pole because he was reading a science fiction book and walking home at the same time.

That concept also is evident in crime victimization profiling. Some teenagers are just more crime prone than others. They don't obey the "rules" of "being alert and being aware."

VICTIM TRAITS

- Victim is unsure, tentative.
- Victim lacks confidence.
- Victim is easily distracted or is already distracted.
- Victim is easily intimidated.
- Victim is overly trusting.
- Another, but opposing, victim trait is the alert, confident student who is reckless and heedless of risk.

Remember the criminals want an "easy" target, a "soft" target. They are looking for an *opportunity* to commit a crime successfully with a *vulnerable* victim, usually someone who is distracted, isolated, and alone. This is the ideal victim. Remember most attackers want an ideal victim, not a fight. Victims have several distinctive traits.

Four Stages of Crime

There are four stages to every crime. These stages create the crime development process. The *first stage* is called surveillance. The student criminal watches other students. He is watching to see what he can steal, who he can bully, and who will be a good target.

The surveillance stage may take just a second or two. Sometimes, however, victims are observed over a long period of time. Sometimes the surveillance lasts for weeks or even months, like when a kidnapper wants to take a child or when a rapist wants to attack a particular girl (sometimes it is a boy). Sometimes the surveillance is intermittent. The surveillant is looking for an opportunity when he is not likely to be identified or arrested. He wants to escape with your money or the items he stole from you. He doesn't want to get caught.

The *second stage* is called an "invitation." The invitation is a distraction. You are walking to school. Someone wants to steal your watch or leather book pack. By engaging you in a conversation, he distracts you and then he stops you. When you are stationary, you are a more likely target. Invitations take many forms. Someone may ask you for change or for directions. "Do you know where Mason Street High School is?" If that is where you are going, say, "Sure, follow me." *But whatever you do, don't stop.* By not stopping, you decrease the likelihood that you will become a crime victim. They expect you to stop, so you throw them off track in terms of their crime plan.

The *third stage* is called a "confrontation." This is initiating "the action" element of the crime. First, they ask you for change or for directions in the invitation. You stop and now they become belligerent. "Only a smart-mouthed kid like you would be able to keep a nice watch like that; I always wanted one, too. Give it to me! Right now!"

FOUR STAGES OF CRIME

- Surveillance
- Invitation
- Confrontation
- Assault

The *fourth stage* is the assault. They start pushing you around, punching you, or steal your watch or ring. Maybe you can get away. Jerk away and run. Try to escape if you can. The easiest avoidance technique, however, occurred before the assault even started. Easy escapes are available between the recognition of the surveillance and the start of the invitation. This is the time where you should turn into a local business, cross the street, or step up on the bus as it pauses at the intersection. Now, this is the time that you should leave. It is hard to change the law or the attitude of your attacker. You may have little or no control over the location of an attack, but you can always use victim avoidance techniques to protect yourself from harm.

Keep your eyes open. Listen! Interpret what you see and hear. If you see a group of gang members or other suspicious persons ahead, decide what to do before you get too close. Perhaps you should alter your direction. By making the right decision, you, too, can avoid becoming a victim.

References

1. Hermann, M. A., and A. Finn. 2002. Professional school counseling: An ethical and legal perspective on the role of school counselors in preventing violence in schools. *Professional School Counseling*, October. http: www.findarticles.com/p/articles/mi_mOKOC/is_1_6/ai_93700939/
2. Chaiet, D., and F. Russell. 1998. *In the safe zone: A kid's guide to personal safety.* New York: Beech Tree, 17.

3

RISK ASSESSMENT

High school student Jerry is concerned about crime in his neighborhood and at school. He is seeing more criminal attack news on TV and is reading more articles in the local paper. There have been more fights at school this year than ever before. Gang colors are very much in evidence and drugs were seized by the police last week. Jerry's dad says that "everything must be all right at Lakeland High or the school authorities would notify us." Mom is not so sure and she is worried about school safety issues.

Jerry wants to know if his school is safe. Is there a problem about security at Lakeland? How can he determine the risk factor? He doesn't want his mom to be worried unnecessarily, but he doesn't want to be caught up in violence because he was unaware. How can he discover whether Lakeland High, its grounds, or the walkways going to and from the school are dangerous? However, it isn't that difficult and you don't have to be a federal agent to figure it out.

Determine Your Risk Factor

The FBI, the state police, and your local police units use complex methods to determine crime risk. But, you don't need to use some convoluted logarithm to determine if you are at risk. Risk assessments can be completed by anyone who is conscientiously committed to obtaining good crime information. To make a risk assessment, you should follow the explanation in the box below.

RISK ASSESSMENT

- Collect crime data at your school and in your neighborhood.

- Make a pin map (1) for all reported crimes. Use colored pins. One color for robbery, another for assault, another for drug sales, etc. Use the pins systematically.
- Make a pin map (2) for the time periods in which crimes occur. Comparing the reported crime map with the time map will give you perspective and context.
- Make a pin map (3) showing the age of those arrested or accused.

You need to know your enemy. A risk assessment program can point the way. Learn where you might be vulnerable. Knowledge is your first line of defense. Knowledge shows you what to do, where to do it, and how to do it. This knowledge can be obtained from your local police department, from the newspapers, radio, or TV broadcasts. Through tabulating summaries of these accounts, you will develop personal and reliable information on which to base security decisions and with which to determine the risk factor.

Making Risk Assessment Maps

Three maps and the crime reports of your city for the past year are all you will need. These maps should depict your home or apartment, your school, and most of the places you frequent during the course of a particular month.

You will need more than one copy of the map because you need to "show" both time, place, and the age of crime victims (and the perpetrators, if known) on your visuals. If the 200 block of Main Street is a drug sale site, a prostitute hangout, and frequently experiences muggings, street robbery, car hijackings, kidnappings, or rape, then you need to know this and you should avoid this neighborhood whenever possible.

You also need to know what time these offenses are occurring. You can easily misrepresent your risk if you use a fact such as: "There were 22 shootings on the 200 block of Main Street last year, therefore, I am at increased risk when I walk down that block." I would avoid the block if I could, just because, sometimes, there are spinoff problems from site violence. However, the 200 block may be relatively safe before school hours, during school hours, or after school hours. It also may become an urban nightmare around midnight.

Hot Spots

There are special places in many neighborhoods and at some schools called "crime zones" or "hot spots." Criminologists know that these are the locations where drug pushers, gang members, Satanists, and weirdo cults hang out. Sometimes the hot spot is a restroom. When this happens, fearful students often stop using these facilities, but needing to use the restroom increases physical discomfort and decreases learning.

Sometimes the hot spot is a particular hallway or a staircase. Informed students may purposefully avoid these areas until after the bell rings, preferring the criticism of their teacher over an attack or a threat by the school bully, a druggie, or a cult member. If a particular restroom or stairway is the hangout for the "rough crowd," go to another restroom or use another stairway, if possible.

When you attended kindergarten or first grade, you were taught to STOP, LOOK, AND LISTEN before crossing the street. You need to do the same thing to avoid crime. You may believe that the police are supposed to keep you safe. To some extent this belief is accurate, but the officers are usually somewhere else when you most need them.

As a state police investigator, co-author Chester Quarles investigated over 200 murders. I never prevented a single killing. I always got there too late. The victim was already dead. Your school security officer will probably be on the other side of the campus when you need him/her the most. Criminals don't normally commit offenses in front of police officers or school administrators. They wait until all adult guardians are out of sight. Because you can't always depend on adults, it becomes your responsibility to avoid crime. Stop, look, and listen was good advice when crossing the street. For crime avoidance purposes you should continue to BE AWARE, LOOK, and LISTEN.

Police officers would call the 200 Block of Main Street a crime "hot spot." Everyone is at increased risk at a crime hot spot. However, if the 22 shootings all occurred after midnight, and none of the shootings occurred immediately before or after school, or during the early evening hours, then the site may not be overly dangerous during much of the day.

It is really easy for your parents to say, "Never ever walk or drive down the 200 block of Main Street." This may be good overall advice, but what happens if you live on that block or just one block over? What if you *must* travel through a crime hot spot to get to school every day? What if you *must* walk by gang, drug, mugger, homeless, and prostitute hangouts? A family may be stuck economically and unable to move, or maybe this location is near a parent's work area, so it saves money to be able to walk versus buying a car or using the city transit service. In this case, the student will need more specific advice.

PINs

A PIN is an imprecise acronym. It stands for Pre-Incident Indicators.[1] Used as a forecasting tool, a PIN can help keep you from harm. A PIN can be based on the actions of others or of a personal observation. Sometimes the PIN comes from a TV, radio, or newspaper report. Some PINs are long range. Some are immediate. Perhaps you have heard that the rival gangs in your school are going to fight next week. This is a strong indicator of impending trouble.

YOUR RISK IS INCREASED WHEN

- Gangs operate with impunity.
- Illegal drug sales are a "growth" business at your school and community.
- Robbers are targeting students at school or near your school.
- Rapists are targeting students at your school or near your school.
- MICAs (Mentally Incompetent, Chemically Addicted persons) frequent your school area.

Steven Fink wrote *Crisis Management: Planning for the Inevitable.*[2] He used the words *prodrome* or *prodromal* to describe precrisis (or precrime) behavior. *Prodrome* is a Greek word meaning "running before." Criminals give us plenty of precrime indicators. The more you can learn about crime in your neighborhood or at your school, the better off you will be.

Some indicators are immediate, however. Let's say that you are walking to school. Knowledge and awareness of your surroundings are critical to PIN usage, so you should always pay attention to what's going on. You spot three gang members standing across the street. You had an argument with one of them last week. You won the verbal dispute and some of your friends laughed at him. He was enraged. He shook his finger in your face and screamed, "I'll get even if it's the last thing I ever do." Now you see him pointing at you.

The three gangsters split up. One walks toward you, another runs ahead, and the third guy rushes over to cut you off from behind. This is a prime example of an immediate threat. You should already be reacting, moving, and avoiding this incident. Maybe you should jump in the empty taxi parked at the curve. Maybe you should step into a local business. If you choose to fight, they will most definitely beat you into pulp unless you are some special hot shot Karate Kid.

Even if you are the Karate Kid, you'll probably be injured in a three on one fight, and even if you win, these guys could come back again, but this time with the whole gang to begin round two of the fight.

Psychologist Gavin DeBecker wrote *The Gift of Fear: Survival Signals That Protect Us from Violence.*[1] He says that "prediction moves from a science to an art when you realize that preincident indicators are *actually part of the incident.* There can be many PINs. A threat may be a PIN. In other cases, a threat might just be a verbal act, mere rhetoric from a verbally aggressive teenager.

When the co-author of this book, Chester Quarles, was 14 years old, a bully telephoned. He said, "I'm coming over to your house to beat you up." Quarles waited all afternoon so that the caller would have his chance. He even cut the grass in the front yard so he would be available. Twice, he watched as the bully rode by on his motorcycle, but he never stopped. His threat was rhetorical hype. Context is very important in terms of your PIN analysis. In his book, DeBecker says that *"context is everything."* We must interpret everything we observe or read about in context. Seeing with your mind as well as with your eyes provides context.

Fear

DeBecker believes very strongly that fear is a basic instinct. Why, on occasion, are we afraid? Why do we feel comfortable around a tattooed 300-pound biker with tattoos, but are intimidated by an 88-pound teenager? The intuition of fear is a benefit of life. Don't be ashamed of being afraid. Listen to your fear. Respond to your fear. Use fear as a forecasting tool.

Let's say that your school is dangerous. If it is, it's dangerous for several reasons. Gangs, drugs, weapons, and student robberies are a part of the daily ritual. Drugs are prevalent. Members of 13 recognized criminal gangs attend your school. There are nearly 2,800 students at your school, representing some 13 language groups and the cultures of over 40 countries.

Police were called seven times during the past three weeks. With all of this disruption, how can you tell which information is important and which is irrelevant? Students are sometimes numbed by their fear because they are frightened so frequently. When this happens, you often go into denial. You become more at risk because you try to persuade yourself that you shouldn't be scared. You need good, accurate, crime information now.

Your risk analysis measurements need to be accurate and precise. You need good information in order to properly assess your school's risk factor and your "personal" risk factor. The term *risk assessment* sounds like an imprecise, vague, scientific term. Fortunately, it's not. The word *risk* applies to all of the possibilities of attack and to all other possible threats.

Receiving and Rating Information

Assessing your risk requires receiving and rating information. There are two different levels of information. One is the eyewitness report. The eyewitness is considered to be a *primary resource.* The witness who overheard someone else's conversation is called a secondary resource. *Secondary resources* are frequently used when gang wars and turf battles are confronted.

AS YOU RECEIVE INFORMATION

- Evaluate the source.
- Evaluate the information.
- Evaluate the consequences of the information.
- Ask for guidance from trustworthy adults.

As you receive information, you will need to evaluate the source, evaluate the information, and evaluate the consequences of the information. This evaluation is vital and necessary for any security analysis or risk assessment. Sometimes you may choose to stay silent on a matter, but if you receive information that your friend Johnny is about to be murdered in a gang initiation, then the consequences of the action require that you *at least* make an anonymous phone call reporting this information. In fact, you should call the police, the principal, and Johnny as well. Wouldn't you want to know if there was a "contract" out on you? You might save Johnny's life. A few weeks from now, he could save yours.

Co-author Tammy Quarles has worked in inner city, suburban, and rural school districts as a certified counselor. She learned early on to develop close working relationships with all of the faculty *and* staff, including administration, teachers assistants, janitors, and grass cutters. Anyone involved in the entire school setting can be a good resource when Johnny is having problems and you are at a loss about the cause.

While the U.S. Secret Service made a major contribution to a national survey of school shooters, they found no precise or specific profile for the violent attackers studied. However, they did discover several warning signs. Fellow students and even teachers who require student papers can help by sharing that certain students are angry and are expressing that anger on paper, drawing, art work, poetry, or notes.[3]

Counselors can help determine if the angry material was written by a bully or someone who is tired of being bullied and is willing to bring a weapon to campus. These events should be carefully investigated and a concise risk assessment should be completed.

A Reliability Index

Once you begin receiving information, you will want to assign a reliability factor to it. Reliable information from a reliable source who has given accurate and dependable information before is given a high rating. Information from someone who is not always dependable may be given an "unknown" rating. Information from someone you do not know at all should be given an even lower rating.

INFORMATION RATING SYSTEM

1. Very reliable information
2. Reliable information
3. Unknown information
4. Suspect information
5. Unreliable information

Very reliable information makes sense and can be verified by another quality source of information. *Reliable* information is consistent with your expectations. It originates with a reliable source and is not in conflict with information you have received from other reliable sources. Unknown information may be an anonymous tip from an unidentified source. It could be in the nature of a phone call, fax, or e-mail. In this case, you won't know the source. *Suspect* information comes from someone you do not know well or perhaps you do know the source well enough to question his or her credibility. Suspect information usually cannot be corroborated by any reliable source. If a violent gang is maliciously spreading false rumors (called *misinformation*), you may find that multiple sources of questionable reliability are spreading the same rumor. Question any information that does not "fit" expectations. *Unreliable* information, on the other hand, may simply come from a source that you do not trust. Unreliable information is usually contradicted by reliable sources and rarely can be verified.

Crime data from your neighborhood indicates what you need to know. It shows you where crimes are occurring. It shows you when crimes are occurring, and the ages of arrested offenders or the probable ages of offenders in the cases not solved. It lets you know who the criminals are and how old they are. Now you can plan an informed response. You can act or react appropriately.

References

1. DeBecker, G. 1997. *The gift of fear: Survival signals that protect us from violence*. New York: Little, Brown Publishers, 98.
2. Fink, S. 1986. *Crisis management: Planning for the inevitable*. New York: American Management Association, 7.
3. Hermann, M. A., and A. Finn. 2002. Professional school counseling: An ethical and legal perspective on the role of school counselors in preventing violence in schools. *Professional School Counseling*, October. http:www.findarticles.com/p/articles/mi_mOKOC/is_1_6/ai_93700939/

4
RISK REDUCTION

Vicki lives in the downtown area. Her mom works in a real estate office and is responsible for several hundred apartment rentals. As part of mom's financial package, they get free rent in a very nice apartment in a building with a doorman. Their apartment building is as safe as any inner city residence can be, but as soon as Vicky steps away from the protection of her building, she walks into a modern urban nightmare.

Vagrants, homeless people, drunks, prostitutes, pimps, gang members, and drug pushers "own" the streets between her apartment and The Center for Art, the unique high school Vicki attends. There are several 24-hour topless bars in the area. Some of Vicki's friends were harassed by guys who thought they were young prostitutes. Some were even hugged and pawed. Embarrassment is the least of their worries and Vicki is scared it will happen to her, too.

She is very careful about how she dresses and makes sure she always carries her school backpack so everyone will know she is a student. She took the "Vicki" tag off the backpack so strangers wouldn't know her name. Vicki wants to find a way to avoid crime, but she doesn't know how. She's asked several of her adult friends, but some of their crime prevention suggestions conflict, so she's not sure that she is getting good advice.

Put the U in Security

> Crimes are prevented all the time. It is a myth that you can't do anything about crime. You can!

If your crime prevention program is going to work, you must learn to avoid, or at least reduce, the risks to your safety and security. Notice that the words *you* and *your* are used repeatedly. This is because you can't take the U out of security. Some cynics might tell you that you really can't avoid crime. "If they really want to get you, they will get you." Often adults, occasionally even a parent, might say that "you can't protect yourself against random acts of violence." These are the most frequently repeated myths. They are believed by many who accept them as some great truth. These myths are usually expressed by people who rarely understand crime. Because the word *ignorance* is defined as "a lack of knowledge or understanding," we can state precisely that these statements are ignorant. You *can* learn to be safe and secure.

Security should be a part of your everyday lifestyle. Since the National School Safety Center indicates that most crimes against children and teenagers occur at school, your school is the single most dangerous place you can go and the incidence of student-on-student and student-on-adult violence has escalated.[1] Of course, a neighborhood bar or a crack house is extremely dangerous, but I am talking about places where "normal" kids go.

Do you know what location is the next most dangerous? No, it is not the entertainment center, the movie theater, the bowling alley, the skating rink, or the local hangout. The next most dangerous place is your home. This is where you probably feel most safe and secure, unless you live in an abusive home. This is where you let your guard down and don't have to live by all these security rules. Right? Wrong! Security must become a part of your security lifestyle both at school, in the community, and at home.

Risks Can Be Managed

MANAGING CRIME RISKS

Remove some risks.
Reduce some risks.
Spread some risks.
Transfer some risks.
Accept risk.

Risks can be managed. Everyone does it to some degree. Your parents may have checking accounts and keep extra money in a bank savings account that has federal insurance, protecting their money against robbery, fraud, or bank failure. Their accounts are much safer than keeping the money at home where you could be invaded, burgled, robbed, or have it lost in a fire.

When your mom holiday shops, she probably puts expensive packages in the trunk rather than inside the car as she continues shopping. This decreases the likelihood of a car burglary because the thief doesn't know if there are valuables there or not. He wants a sure thing. If she put the package on the back seat, she might loose a window as well as the package.

Risk removal for a teenager could involve leaving an expensive watch at home, for example. If your dad's expensive notebook computer is likely to be taken, he should leave it at home. If you have an expensive jacket, it is preferable that you wear an inexpensive one to school. Risk removal also can save your life.

> Reducing the amount of cash you take to school each day lowers the possibility that you will be a crime victim.

If you have $100 cash in your wallet, risk reduction means that you should take only enough for your daily needs. Leave the rest at home or in your bank account. Risk reduction significantly influences whether you will be selected for a crime. Risk reduction is also a good crime prevention and risk management technique. Reducing the amount of money you take to school each day helps protect you from harm.

Risk spreading also lowers your risk. Let's say you are going to the bank after school today. You have $100 in cash. You put $25 in each of your four trouser pockets. If someone robs or mugs you, the person usually reaches for the wallet. He may get the wallet and the $25 in it, but he won't get all your cash because he won't look in the other pockets. This is a good example of risk spreading.

Risk transference is another technique. One example is in purchasing an insurance policy. Another example is when a store transfers money to an armored car, which moves the loss risk to the armored car company instead of the store. A good example of personal risk transference could be between family members. Younger brother Bobby has had his lunch money stolen twice, so big brother carries the cash and gives it to Bobby's teacher. The larger brother then accepts the risk.

All crime cannot be removed, reduced, spread, or transferred. Some crime risks just have to be accepted. Banks may be robbed, but very few close their doors because of robbery. Convenience stores and liquor stores have a very high risk factor, but you find them in almost every part of town. Many stores are open 24 hours a day. This increases their risk.

Some risk has to be accepted. All risk can never be eliminated. So, you do the best you can, but you do your best conscientiously. You practice the principles of crime deterrence, crime avoidance, and crime prevention.

Students who observe bullying behavior also suffer consequences and tend to view their school in a negative way or see it as an unsafe environment. In a worst-case scenario, they may become fearful for their own safety. Counselors can teach the guidelines on how to respond to threats and how to stay safe. And, this information can be constantly reinforced in counseling sessions, giving students confidence when they must deal with a bully.

Managing Your Risk

You may not be able to eliminate all risk in your life, but you can influence that risk. There are several things you can do to influence risk. One thing you cannot afford to do is to ignore the risk and hope that it will go away. This is like the ostrich who hides his head in the sand hoping the lion won't attack. Ignoring the crime risk in America is not an appropriate option. Whatever the risk, you *must* deal with it. The ostrich method leads to injury and possible death.

CRIME PREVENTION APPROACHES

Do Nothing

- You ignore the risk.

Do Something

- You can reduce the risk.
- You can transfer the risk.
- You can remove the risk.

One crime prevention approach is to reduce the risk. You can reduce the risk by reading this book, by becoming aware of risk, and by learning how to deal with the risk. Risk reduction increases your security. It makes everyone in the vicinity safer because of your precautions.

One of the first murders co-author Chester Quarles was associated with as a young criminal investigator involved the killing of a 16-year-old girl. Tragically, she was just in the wrong place at the wrong time. Her parents told her not to visit a particular night spot featuring live entertainment, dancing, and beer.

She and her boyfriend wanted to hear the new band, so they disobeyed the parents. They just bought a cola and were having a good time, until a gunfight broke out between a man, his wife, and her boyfriend. The boyfriend missed his self-defense shot, but drilled the 16-year–old teenager. She was dead before she hit the ground. The cause of death was gunshot wound, but the reason for her death was that she didn't obey her parents.

Join with Other Students

While risks can be ignored, the most appropriate response is risk reduction. Risks also may be reduced when other students join with you in an effort to ensure safety for all. Security is your concern. A safe school has many benefits. You will enjoy being at a safe school. You will be better able to concentrate on your studies.

Risk transference is another approach. It works in many ways. The bully and the thief are transferred from a regular school to an alternative school. Gang members are redistributed among several other schools. Perhaps a dozen teenagers are wearing their gang colors and are intimidating nonmembers. The gangs occasionally even threaten teachers.

In a large school district, these fellows (and their sisters and girl-friends) may be transferred to other schools. So, instead of having 12 members of the "Bumblebee Mafia" at one school, there are only two members at six different schools. Sometimes this doesn't work because these gangsters recruit new members at their new schools. Maybe some of these kids will be sent to the state youth prison. This is a *real* transfer.

Risk removal is the last approach. You can stop taking nonessential monies or personal property to school. You can stay home today because a gang member threatened you. There are 800,000 kids who stay home from school every year because of criminal threats.[2] Oftentimes, it is the appropriate thing to do.

Are You a Target?

There are several crime deterrence and crime prevention terms that you should understand. The first term is *a soft target*. A soft target is an easy target. The next term you should remember is *target hardening*. Target hardening makes it much more difficult for someone to commit a crime. Target hardening increases the risk for the criminal. He or she is much more likely to be seen, identified, and arrested for committing the crime. Let's look carefully at the concept of a soft and a hard target.

A Soft Target

Suzy brought $300 to school today. She is excited about clothes shopping with her mom this afternoon, so she tells all her friends what she will be doing and that the money is in her purse. She has her lunch money in her pocket, as is appropriate. During lunch, however, she leaves her purse, with the $300 inside, inside her homeroom. Suzy and her $300 are a soft target. It will be an easy crime. Johnny is an experienced and successful thief and has been stealing since he was four years old. He isn't bright enough to finish his algebra homework, but he knows how to add Suzy's cash to his bankroll. Hearing her discussion, he eats quickly and sneaks back to the homeroom, which is empty. As surreptitious as a cat burglar, he steals Suzy's money.

Moving quickly to the restroom, he hides the money inside his socks, He is walking on the money now. He figures that even if he should become a suspect that the principal will just search his pockets and book bag. He knows school administrators can get in trouble when they search a teen, and it would take a strip search to find the $300. Johnny doesn't need to worry, however. Suzy won't even realize she has been victimized until she is ready to pay for the really nice outfit she and her mom find at the mall.

A Hard Target

Jimmy Smith's dad just bought an exceptionally expensive notebook computer. Mr. Smith is an engineer and runs all sorts of complex mathematical equations through his notebook. The laptop cost $8,300 and the math/science/engineering software cost another $3,600. He has nearly $12,000 invested in the new notebook and its programs.

Mr. Overby, Jimmy's Calculus II teacher, upon learning about this exceptional computer, asked Jimmy to bring the computer to school for a demonstration. Mr. Overby called Jimmy's dad and carefully worked out secure arrangements for this valuable piece of property.

First, Jimmy rides to school with his mom, instead of taking the bus. The computer notebook is in his backpack along with his books. The demonstration has not been previously announced, so this supercomputer is a surprise. Mr. Overby is waiting for Jimmy at the school entrance. As Jimmy exits from the car, the calculus teacher takes the computer to the teachers' lounge and secures the notebook in his personal locker with a quality padlock. The teachers' lounge can only be entered through the reception area of the principal's office; students do not have access.

This is a good example of target hardening. Several security issues were confronted. First, those involved planned for a risk. In fact, Jimmy's dad even purchased computer insurance, so even if the computer was stolen or destroyed, he would not lose all of his financial investment. The second security measure was to ensure that the computer was promptly taken by Mr. Overby, a teacher and a responsible adult. It is no longer in Jimmy's care. Third, the computer notebook was placed in a secured locker in the teachers' lounge. Only teachers can enter, and Mr. Overby protects his locker with a quality lock. All of these efforts would be included in the concept of target hardening. Jimmy's dad plans to come by the school on his way home from work and Mr. Overby will personally return the computer. Jimmy will go home on the bus, but without the computer.

Could someone steal the notebook? Of course, but it would be very difficult and there would be a very high risk. There was very little risk, however, on the $300 theft from Suzy's purse by Johnny. He just walked into an empty classroom and took what he wanted.

Jimmy Smith, his dad, and Mr. Overby planned to minimize their risk. Their preparation increased the security for the computer notebook. Suzy didn't make any arrangements at all. Then she bragged about the shopping trip to all of her friends. Suzy never had anything stolen from her before, so she believes that everyone in her class is just as honest as she is. Because she was so trusting, she doesn't realize that her money was gone until she's tried on a cute outfit that fits perfectly. She won't be buying it today. In fact, she left the store in tears.

Taking money to school, especially larger sums, is always risky. However, Suzy could have lowered her risk by remaining silent about the money and by not mentioning the shopping trip. She also could have put the money in a small wallet or money clip in the front pocket of her jeans. She could tell about the trip the next day, while she shows off her new clothes. At the very least, she should have taken her purse with her wherever she went. Probably the best option would have been for her mother to hold the money in safekeeping. Each of these steps would have increased Suzy's personal security and protected the $300 from being stolen. Each of these actions would be good examples of target hardening.

Friendliness

Students who are friendly are less likely to be attacked by a young criminal. Look at other students. Smile and greet them as a friend.

"Hi, how are you today?" This simple statement is friendly, but also is a crime prevention technique. There were 12 dead and 23 wounded in the attack at Littleton, Colorado's Columbine High School in 1999, but there were students who were not targeted as well. The killers walked by several students they liked without pulling a trigger. Seventeen-year-old Brooks Brown's life was spared even though he was one of the first students to be confronted by the killers. When he came face-to-face with Eric Harris, he was instructed, "Brooks, I like you, now get out of here. Go home!" Being friendly to others, especially "outsiders," can save your life.

> Students who are friendly are less likely to be attacked by criminals.

Look at them when you greet them. Make brief eye contact and nod at them. However, don't maintain this eye contact. Some gang members might interpret this as an insolent, nonverbal challenge. A stare could be easily misunderstood. Many gangs use a stare to intimidate others. A stare is especially inappropriate for girls because a creepy guy may think you want a date or you are interested in him. However, a brief look, a smile, and a nod is a crime deterrent. You are merely being polite, but you also are indicating that you noticed that person.

Psychologists tell us that these are subliminal messages. A subliminal message communicates, "I noticed you and I can identify you in a police lineup." Identifying *who* is the most important part of your crime prevention quest. Keep your eyes on the *who*. No one was ever attacked, robbed, or raped by a what, why, where, when, or how. "Oh, I know that nice people don't think that way, but delinquents do." A nonthreatening, subliminal message can even save your life.

> Look, but don't stare at those around you.

If the guy Cindy just looked at and said "hi" to was planning to steal Cindy's purse, he probably just changed his mind. Why? Because Cindy can place him at the crime scene during the time period that the theft occurred. This is dangerous to him. It is a significant risk. Even though he wants the money, he does not want to be labeled as a thief. He doesn't want to be suspected, either. He's not a strong-armed robber, he wants to remain anonymous; he's a "sneak" thief.

Last, but not least, he doesn't want to be caught. He doesn't want to be arrested. He wants to be trusted, so he feels comfortable in stealing again in the same room. Because you saw him and you can place him at the scene, he probably will not steal today.

You can make a difference at school. Crime rates can be influenced positively anywhere. Crimes can't be influenced when you do not help deter or prevent them. Never let your guard down. Everyone should implement good security practices. Vigilance should be the first approach.

Let's say that a bully named Billy abuses young kids, intimidates teenagers, and frequently throws "fits." When he gets mad, he fights just about anybody who is around. Billy's crimes are right there for all to see. Lots of kids are so afraid of Billy that they keep silent about his crimes, privately hoping that he won't bother them. Billy's crimes, (abuse, drug pushing, and stealing from younger kids) are secret.

They are secret because the kids are so afraid of Billy that they haven't told the principal, the counselor, or the police about his crimes. The secrecy allows Billy to maintain power. Try to figure out a way that you can solve this security dilemma without having to confront Billy. Develop a plan to ensure that the police are involved.

In some cities, this is relatively easy. Let's say that Billy carries a switchblade knife or a pistol to school. He uses the weapon to threaten young kids and other teenagers. A switchblade is illegal in any state, but any knife is illegal at school. Most schools have an expulsion policy—bring a gun or knife to school and you are expelled for a year. You are arrested and prosecuted before the juvenile court as well. This is the way you "remove" Billy. The next time you know he has the knife, call the principal's office anonymously if you are afraid to make a personal complaint.

Some cities have Crime Stopper programs. Memphis, Tennessee, and Albuquerque, New Mexico, run school Weapons Watch programs under their Crime Stopper Programs. Students who see weapons at school are awarded $50 anonymously. Wouldn't this be wonderful? You get rid of the gun and you get rid of Jimmy, a member of the Bandito gang; Billy, the bully; and Johnny, the drug pusher, who have all been carrying guns and you get the reward money, too. Actually, you get a double award: the money and their dismissal from school.

These gangsters won't be bothering anyone for quite a while. This, too, is a satisfying feeling.

Perhaps you should call the police. In the State of Washington, you can call 1-800-862-GUNS (all calls are confidential). After installing this free-call hotline, authorities quickly reported an average of 187 calls each school day. These calls came from all over the state and included large, small, city, suburban, and rural schools. When an anonymous phone call goes into the Washington State Guns Hotline, police authorities respond immediately.

The police will probably bring a dog capable of smelling guns and drugs. They will check Billy's book bag and his locker as well as letting the dog "screen" the area. If Billy is using a weapon or drugs, he goes to jail and he doesn't come back to your school. He doesn't even get to know who "informed." Billy is removed as a threat, possibly to never return again. He will be transferred to an alternative school for delinquents, not your school. He won't even get to be a bully at the alternative school because there is usually one teacher for each five or six students.

Knowledge is power. Use your knowledge for your own safety and the safety of your friends. Students often become so accustomed to their school security technology that they forget about the fact that closed circuit television (CCTV) units were installed at their school last year. At one school, students who were being "extorted" (their lunch money was being taken) arranged to stand in front of the school camera when "their" thief arm-twisted, socked, and stole. It appeared that the "theft in front of the camera" was accidental, but it wasn't. It was a setup, carefully arranged by his victims.

Now, this is not a crime known as "entrapment." You are just arranging for a thief and bully to steal from you in front of the camera and not down the hall or on the school yard. The principal comes out and gets Billy. It looks like it was coincidental, but it wasn't. Set up *your* bully! Think how pleasant that experience would be. Sherlock Homes or Colombo couldn't do a better job and your bully will have self-destructed. He will have a new nickname. It won't be Billy "Bully" anymore; it will be Billy "Dummy" now, the idiot who committed a crime for all to see right in front of the TV camera.

References

1. Blauvelt, P. D. 1999. *Making schools safe for students: Creating a proactive school safety plan.* Thousand Oaks, CA: Corwin Press, 1.
2. Landen, W. 1994. Violence and our schools: What can we do? In *Creating safe schools: What principals can do,* ed. M. S. Hill and F. W. Hill, 42. Thousand Oaks, CA: Corwin Press.

5

YOUR PERSONAL
SECURITY PROGRAM

Rhonnie lives in a neighborhood about three blocks from her school. Jenny lives near her and they usually walk to school together. In years past, neither of the girls felt uncomfortable in their school walk, but things seem different this year. The quickest route to school takes them right past some gangster-looking guys who make Rhonnie feel very uncomfortable. She doesn't like the way they stare and she thinks they are mumbling inappropriate remarks, but she can't hear them clearly, so she isn't sure.

She is apprehensive, however. Chill bumps went down her spine the last time she and Jenny came in contact with the gangsters. Rhonnie wants to take another route, so they don't have to pass these creeps every day. Jenny disagrees. "The way we are going is the most direct route and we know those guys from school," she says. "Everything will be all right. Don't worry." Their argument was intense, so both girls chose their own individual routes the next day. Each went alone.

Rhonnie walked to school without incident, but Jenny was crying when they met for first period. The group of guys had surrounded Jenny when she was alone, making inappropriate remarks. They asked her if she was a virgin and wanted to know if she would date their leader. They were crude and very vivid in their descriptions about how Jenny's jeans fit and how snug her sweater was.

Her dress habits are very modest, but Jenny felt cheap after they had talked about her body. After Jenny ran away, she became frightened about what could have happened that morning and what might happen in the future. Rhonnie and Jennie always walk the alternate route together now and they have had no further incidents.

Sara lives in a small farm community. Everybody knows everybody for miles around. She has always felt safe and secure as well. Her folks felt that she was safe, so they let her walk nearly three miles to school every day. She is alone for over half of her walk. Yesterday, on a lonely stretch, a stranger pulled up beside her and asked for directions. He said he had a map and asked her to show him the way to a local farm. She wanted to help, so she walked over to his car. When she looked in, however, she didn't see a map at all. All she could see was that this guy was naked from the waist down; he only had on a T-shirt. Sara screamed and ran home. Her folks were glad that the pervert didn't grab her while she was most vulnerable (very close to his car). Sara knows that she will never walk up close to a stranger's car again.

Be Careful

If you were on tour in an African jungle or a Latin American swamp, you probably would be very careful about stepping on snakes or into quicksand. We are afraid of those things we don't know much about. As tourists, we might not have the skills necessary to avoid either of these risks. However, right here at home, we often "deny" our risks. We have gotten so used to our risks that we do not even consciously consider them anymore.

How many teens step off the curb quickly when the traffic light changes in their favor? Yet, is it not possible that the approaching driver has defective brakes, is inattentive, or drunk and will not stop? Is it not possible that by stepping out without looking both ways, that you increase the likelihood of a collision or a hit and run? Many young people just step right out into high crime-rate districts just as casually. They walk into big-time trouble without seeing it in advance. You need to be able to *see* if you are going to avoid trouble, if you are going to be secure.

Never Delegate Your Security

The word *delegation* means to appoint or assign someone else to represent you. Sometimes we do this politically, but it is a very poor idea to delegate in terms of personal protection. It is very easy to say, "I don't have to worry about crime. That's what we have policemen for. It is *their* job to protect me." With an attitude like this, you can rest assured that you will become one of every four citizens who are victimized by a serious crime within the next four years.

Co-author Chester Quarles was a police officer and later served as a criminal investigator. "I never investigated a rape, a murder, a robbery, or an arson that hadn't *already happened*. People who depended on me to prevent their crime or to protect them from crime were tragically disappointed. I did all I could, but I never prevented even one of these crimes."

For you to believe that officers will protect you when you need them is an unreasonable expectation. It is a *myth* to believe that you can always depend on the police, or anyone else. A police officer won't be there when you are frightened. He probably won't be close enough to hear you scream. It is *your* responsibility to avoid crime, to deter crime, and to prevent crime.

Personal Security

Personal security is the simple act of accepting responsibility for your own safety. You accept this responsibility just as you accept other responsibilities. The *total* responsibility for your own safety is yours. There are steps that governments and institutions should take, but they can make mistakes or commit errors. Therefore, most of the time you won't be able to depend on anyone but yourself.

Everyone should have a personal security program. Locking your house or car is a good example. Locking your clothes, watch, and money in a locker at the gym is another example. At home, a barking dog is also a good crime deterrent. Likewise, there are many things you can do before school, on the way to school, at school, and on the way home to increase your safety and decrease your risk.

You need a security plan and you need a security program. Patrick Collins, a former CIA operative who served in many dangerous countries, wrote a book, *Living in Trouble Lands*. He recommended that everyone design their own personal security program.

> A personal security program is the simple act of protecting oneself from harm. It is the accumulation of the actions you have taken throughout your lifetime to reduce or eliminate the chances of being assaulted,

attacked, beaten, molested, raped or murdered. You practice personal security to varying degrees every day of your life.[1]

A personal security program is the simple act of protecting yourself from physical harm. Your security program is a "target hardening approach." Remember, a hard target is a difficult target (see Chapter 4). An easy target or victim is a "soft" one. Teenagers who become target hardened are much less likely to be victimized. In its most ideal form, a target-hardened individual is simply overlooked. It is as if the crook never even sees this person as a target. They see someone else instead.

While you need a security plan, you also need to develop two personal behavioral characteristics into high-level skills. These include: the characteristic of the *gift of observation* and the characteristic of *mental alertness.* "Now everybody sees," you say. "Everybody observes." Yes and no.

Be Alert

The truly observant person is mentally alert. He or she is aware of unsafe areas and is aware that some relatively safe locations are dangerous at specific times. The very best crime avoidance strategy is to be aware. A perfectly safe location at 8 a.m. may be incredibly dangerous at midnight. Observant students are always examining *and interpreting* their surroundings. They look, they see, they "feel," they interpret, they detect, and they avoid problems for themselves and others. They create the impression of self-confidence and self control. They trust their instincts because their instincts are finely tuned.

They look—*really look*—as they walk down school hallways or as they sit down at lunch. As you walk school hallways, you need to look at each student you pass. Try to gain just a moment of eye contact. Don't stare them down; staring is considered to be aggressive behavior. Guys fight other guys over stare games. Just glance at other students when you walk by. When possible, greet them. Be friendly. The eye contact should not be intimidating or challenging. Staring will raise your crime risk, if the viewer thinks you are challenging him or her.

However, you have accomplished something by looking at the other student and greeting that person. You sent what psychologists call a subliminal message. The message is basically this: "I saw you. I recognize you. I can identify you." This is a powerful restraint on the part of the individual offender, especially at a public school. Predators tend to avoid those who look like they may respond assertively. They want meek and quiet victims, not someone who will yell or fight, so they pick on people who are texting on their cell phones, listening to headsets, and not paying attention. If you have the tendency to stare down at the floor when you feel bad or depressed, work on remedying this habit. You will be safer when you stop this behavior.

In many cases, victims attract the attention of predators because of the way they walk, talk, or dress. The student who is afraid, walking with her head down, is an inviting target. Students who send a message that they are shy, insecure, uncoordinated, or lack confidence reassure the criminal. While wealth and really nice clothes, jewelry, or watches increase the likelihood of being targeted, criminals do not always choose the affluent. They choose the first suitable victim available.

Be Friendly to All

Be friendly to all. This is not the superficial friendliness of somebody running for student council office. It is the consistent friendliness that comes naturally to many people. Friendliness offers many social advantages, not the least of which increases your safety.

Friendly students are less likely to be molested. Bullies and the gangs usually bother students they don't like or respect. If you are popular and well liked, you are less likely to be attacked. Loners and students who are disliked are at higher risk.

Vigilance

The gifts of being aware—observation skills and precriminal activity interpretation—are necessary in any security plan. Vigilance is another. Vigilance simply means to stay alert or aware and be watchful for trouble. In truly dangerous schools, you must always be vigilant, even in the classroom, but your primary threats are in the hallways, the cafeteria, the gym, the rest rooms, and the school yard. More school murders and the more serious assaults occur in the lunchroom than at any other school location.

Vigilant students never let anyone get close enough to them to compromise their activities. They do not walk alone or unescorted through dangerous areas or in any areas unsupervised by guardians. Robberies, assaults, and rapes increase when potential victims are inattentive and careless. Vigilance and care lowers your risk considerably.

TARGET HARDENING

- Learn about crime in your area.
- Be vigilant.
- Observe your environment at all times. Look for threats continuously.
- *React immediately.* Don't even think about it. If you see a threat or a risk, do what the military does. Take *countermeasures* immediately.

Crime avoidance should become a way of life. It is based on certain skills, the most important of which is continual observation and awareness. Be wary. Always watch for danger. Keep up with the crime trends in your neighborhood and at your school. When you know how the crime occurs, when it occurs, and how it occurs, you have several more tactics or tools available in your crime avoidance toolkit.

Reference

1. Collins, P. 1991. *Living in troubled lands.* Boulder, CO: Paladin Press.

6

EVERYDAY SECURITY DECISIONS

Jodie and her brother, Jim, attend Bigsville High. The school is named appropriately because it is one, huge complex. There are 5,600 children, youth, and teenagers who arrive on this campus 5 days a week, 10 months a year. The school board thought it was more "efficient" to bring everyone together in one central complex. They thought that neighborhood schools were too expensive. There are separate buildings for the elementary, middle, and high school, but every student must come together in the traffic pick-up lines, the parking lots, the bus zone, and the cafeteria.

The school has grown by leaps and bounds, as more and more new students have transferred in. The cozy, little-town atmosphere is now lost at Bigsville High, which is just a warehouse for kids— lots of them. And the school board thinks that big classes are okay, too. There are 35 to 40 students in every class. "It saves money," they say.

So, Jodie and Jim are stuck in an impersonal environment, a school that is too big. This is a school where the teachers are so stressed out and tired that they spend all of their time working with the very best students or the very worst students. The guys and gals in the middle must succeed or fail on their own. Lots of students are angry, rebellious, and hostile. They aren't getting a good education and they know it. Their futures are at stake because only the best students will pass the college entrance exams. There are no gangs here and the school is relatively drug free. There are just too many people and too much tension. Fights break out frequently.

How do Jodie and Jim plan for their own safety? What decisions must they make each day to stay safe at school? Deciding what they wear, what they take with them or leave behind, and how they are going to act is all very important.

Deciding on What to Wear

Clothing that reflects "you" and your personality can be distinctive. When you dress in "your colors" and "your styles," you look good and feel better about yourself. The cost of your clothes, however, influences crime prevention. You should never wear "too much" wealth. Picture this scenario in any upscale school. Jack is wearing $200 Nikes, $135 designer jeans, a $78 shirt, and a $200 NFL game day jacket. He has an $850 sports watch, a $900 gold chain around his neck, and a $500 gold-braid wristlet.

Louise is wearing an ensemble that cost $375 and a leather-sleeved school letter jacket costing $345. Her watch, earrings, bracelet, anklet, and necklace are valued at over $1,500. Dominic is wearing a full-length leather coat valued at $750 and a $1,100 gold necklace.

Each of these young people is "at risk." In other words, Jack, Louise, and Dominic have a much higher likelihood of being robbed than any of their friends. Louise is also more likely to be raped. Once she has been cut off and isolated for the robbery, the offender may decide to take more than her valuables. Always remember that your clothing, accessories, or jewelry may be the initial attraction, which singles you out as a criminal target.

Whenever you wear clothing that attracts the eye of your friends, you also attract the eye of criminals, creeps, and delinquents. Designer jeans, expensive jackets, leather apparel, and costly sports shoes lower your level of safety in today's world. The clothing is like a crime magnet. Co-author Quarles' five children wore clothing purchased at the local Walmart, Kmart, or Big K. If we lived in other sections of the United States, we would have picked some other value stores in which to shop. The children were safer this way, but we really didn't have any other choice. Walmart was the best we could do.

The Question of School Uniforms

Many schools now require uniforms. This eliminates the economic class distinctions of the poorer versus the wealthier student. It reduces the stigma of wealth. It also eliminates some of the "gang" colors, which are quite present in many schools. The uniform lowers the likelihood of a sneak thief targeting your locker or gym basket. (Who would want to steal a school uniform?) It lowers the risk of criminal attack in any form, by any other student at that school.

If your school does not have uniforms, you should dress comfortably, but inexpensively. I know that designer jeans are preferred, but discount clothing stores sell clothing that will fit well and you can find colors and styles for shirts, jeans, blouses, and dresses that will reflect favorably upon your personality. Be careful when selecting clothing. This is one time you need to think like a thief, a crook, or a rapist. If you pick a red, black, or some other vivid color, will you be at a higher risk?

Teenagers wearing bright clothing are easily noticed. Girls wearing skin-tight clothes or micro-mini skirts are always spotted. In fact, in a crowd, they are always noticed first. You don't want to be noticed "first" by a criminal or a juvenile delinquent. Don't let a crook's eye stop on you. Dress in the same colors as everyone else and you won't stand out. What you wear and carry with you can identify you as an easy target. Conversely, your clothing also can signal that you are a more difficult target.

What you wear and what you carry can make it easier to fend off an attacker or to escape. Dress more for defense than for looks. You can run faster in tennis shoes, than in loafers, boots, or heels. Also loose-fitting slacks are better for running or self-defense.

Don't Let His Eye Stop on You

Test the concept: Don't let a crook's eyes stop on you. Go up to a second or third floor of a school or downtown building. Look out a window facing the sidewalk. Watch the people walking by. Who do you look at first? Who do you look at twice? Who do you look at longer? Why did these particular people attract your attention? The reason requires some speculation, but it also requires careful analysis.

> - The safest person on the street is someone who looks and dresses like everyone else.
> - The person with the highest risk is dressed uniquely or carries obvious wealth.
> - Anonymity is an advantage as a crime-prevention tactic.

In this exercise, think like a thief, a robber, or even a rapist. Quite often the eye stops on someone who dresses differently or wears bright colors or unique styles of clothing. Sometimes a behavioral characteristic or peculiarity is what "stops" the criminal eye. The safest person on the street is someone who looks like most others of his/her age or sex. The person who "stands out" because of clothing is more likely to be victimized. Anonymity is an advantage in this respect.

This same philosophy should reflect your posture and the way you walk. Timid, shy people are much more likely to become crime victims. The young person who walks erect, pulls his or her shoulders back, and "watches" the environment is less likely to become a victim. The person who has poor posture, looks down as he or she walks, and does not observe the surroundings is an excellent victim and is much more likely to be attacked.

Size, weight, and age may be important factors when crooks select their next target, but these factors are much less important than most students believe. A feisty seven-year-old girl may project the image that she will not be a good target while a "head-in-clouds," 19-year-old mush brain nerd sends out the message that he will be a great target.

Girls, remember that criminals make their decisions to attack based on sight and intuition. They attack on reflex, like a fish snapping at bait. If you are walking to a friend's apartment dressed in shorts or a mini skirt and a tank top, or a skin-tight exercise suit, you can be assured that many eyes are stopping on you, appraising you. The eye stops on bright clothes, tight-fitting clothes, and immodest hem or bust lines. Most of these appraisals are innocent. Guys are finding you attractive and other girls are wishing they were as pretty as you. Some of these observers, however, may be criminals. Many of these guys are creeps. Moreover, some of these viewers may even be rapists. Don't dress so extravagantly or immodestly that the eye *always* stops on you. It just isn't safe, for boys or girls.

Women of the Middle East were very modest in their dress code. In fact, many still are, except for those who have adapted Western dress standards. While these standards may sound like they are nearly 2,000 years old (and they are), they still send the message that women who dress modestly are safer in dangerous environments.

Knowing How to Walk

The way you dress is not the only crime victimization problem. The way you walk is important as well. Walking as an achiever is important. You want to send a positive, nonverbal message to everyone that you will *not* be a good crime victim. A negative or passive message sends a signal that you will be a good victim, so watch your environment, pull your shoulders back, and walk with an obvious purpose. It is an assertive posture and a healthy one. Do not "affect" a woman's walk. High heels accentuate an ultrafeminine walk, but a sensual stroll is dangerous. Don't display your figure by a pronounced walk. Guys will notice you without these obvious affectations.

To send the subliminal message—"I will not be a good or easy crime victim"—you need to walk erect and with confidence. You also need to walk strategically. If there are no students in the hallway, the safest route is in the center of the hall. If someone initiates a confrontation, you can move in more directions. You are not likely to be pinned against the wall, unless you were not being observant.

When changing classes, your safest location would be to the right, adjacent to the wall. You are more vulnerable when students are both to your right and to your left. You also are more vulnerable if you are adjacent to students moving in the opposite direction. You are *less* vulnerable when all the students adjacent to your space are moving in the same direction.

Deciding on What to Take with You and What to Leave Behind

Clothing is a strong component in anyone's crime prevention arsenal. The right clothes decrease your victimization probability. The wrong clothes increase the likelihood of your being targeted by a criminal. This isn't all, however. There are many "possessions" that increase your likelihood of being targeted. One is an iPod. Anyone listening to music has significantly restricted his/her hearing. You can't hear the street gang approaching from behind. You can't hear the out-of-control vehicle. So, the music lovers become crime or accident statistics and these are the ones you hear about on TV or read about in the newspaper.

You should not take anything to school that you do not need. If art class is only on Friday afternoons, you do not need to take the art book with you every day, unless you plan a special review during study hall. Every additional book decreases your ability to flee and to react. Leaving the extra books at home or in your locker also minimizes your loss should you be targeted by a thief.

Most of the junk in your book bag, attaché, or purse could be left at home. Take what you need, but leave the rest behind. Sometimes you take things that increase your risk and the likelihood you will be targeted by a criminal. Let's say you are going to a math class. Your dad's calculator may increase the likelihood that you will be victimized, especially if there are only two or three calculators in the room.

If everyone has a simple, inexpensive, basic calculator, your multifunctional trigonometric, calculus, and engineering model may be the best and most expensive in the room or even in the entire school. By carrying the fancy model, you significantly increase the likelihood that you will be targeted. The same thing is true of computer notebooks and electronic recordkeeping aids. They are nice, but, because these same items are frequently stolen at your dad's and mom's workplace, they will certainly be tempting in a school environment.

Girls, take a good look at your purse. Do you really need all that junk? When was the last time you used that purple-tinted, sequined lip ice? Do you always put your money in your purse or could you use a wallet like the guys do? You should put your money in your pocket. If somebody wants the wallet badly enough, just throw it down and run. The robber probably just wants the money.

Because you plan to "throw the wallet," you shouldn't leave anything in it that you can't lose. This also applies in a purse snatching. If somebody grabs your purse and runs, you won't lose everything because you've already transferred your cash to a wallet. Buy a small, inexpensive cloth wallet that doesn't protrude like a leather fold-over does. It won't "show" or be noticeable. Because the wallet is in your pocket, you won't lose too much if your purse is snatched. You curtailed your loss by behaving appropriately and by living a crime avoidance lifestyle.

FOR GIRLS ONLY

- Carry your purse closed.
- Secure your purse with a strap.
- Keep your money in your pocket.
- Keep your car keys in your pocket.
- Keep your house keys in your pocket.
- If somebody grabs your purse, let them have it. Then RUN and YELL.

There are other things you need to consider when you decide what to take with you and what you leave behind. You can buy a quality canvas or leather-bottomed book pack for less than $40. Should you use the $250 leather book satchel your grandma gave you for your birthday? I would think long and hard before making that decision. Somebody may take your book bag and all that is in it, just because you took an expensive one to school.

The same thing is true of a brief case or attaché. You can buy a good one for $30 or less. Do you really need to take the leather case your dad doesn't use? You know, the one imported from Colombia, South America, that retails for $850 here in the United States. The decision you make on the attaché or a more expensive backpack may be one of the most important decisions you will ever make. If you make the wrong choice, it may even be the last decision you ever make.

Street Crime Alarms

There are several types of street robbery alarms that you can use, or you can purchase a police whistle. These noisemakers are excellent defensive weapons. Personal alarms and whistles are most effective in crowds. You can even put one in your purse or attaché and loop the pull-chord over your wrist. If someone snatches your book bag, the security chord is separated from the alarm. Some of these make a tremendous noise.

One really expensive security attaché (it costs more than $3,000) has a mild electrical charge. A thief steals your dad's security attaché and hears an ear-piercing alarm. If the thief doesn't put the attaché down quickly, he or she will suddenly feel a powerful and disabling electrical charge surging through his or her body.

Sears and Radio Shack stores sell a boat horn small enough to fit in a purse, fanny pack, or backpack. About the size of your dad's travel-size shaving cream aerosol, it has a plastic horn attached. It costs less than $10, but it's nearly as loud as an 18 wheeler's air horn. If you need crime-influencing attention in an emergency, you'll surely get it with the boat horn.

Learn to "Power" Yell

A scream is a weak-sister compared to a power yell. A scream is often compulsive and panic-driven. The power yell is controlled, vibrant, and is the loudest noise that a human can make. The yell comes from deep inside. You have to practice this yell to get it right. You yell as long as it's to your advantage. The moment it isn't, or a gun or knife is the penalty if you don't stop, then you can alter your response to another approach.

Communication Systems

Another weapon is a communication system. A cellular telephone is the best weapon you can have. If you have one, take it with you whenever possible. Because the phone itself could be a crime target, you should keep the instrument in a book pack or purse. Unfortunately, many schools do not allow cellular phones at school. Incoming calls are disruptive. Many of the young people who first used them at school were dope dealers getting their next illegal order. Unless you are walking through a metal detector each day, you can carry your cellular unit undetected, if you turn it off for all incoming calls.

In other words, you can call out during an emergency. Now don't misunderstand. The mere possession of a cellular phone is often against school policy. Certainly, you can't receive any personal calls while you are at school, but wouldn't you rather be disciplined and be safe than not be safe at all? When you are walking past the gang bangers, your cell phone will be there with you. A personal communication system is very reassuring, even for a police officer. Get one if you can.

If someone bothers you on the way to, or from, school, all you need to do is dial your emergency number. Call the cellular equivalent to 911 in most dialing districts in the United States for immediate police, fire, or ambulance service. Just calling out can decrease your risk if someone is bothering you. They see you make the call and leave before officers arrive.

Weapons or Pepper Spray

We do not *ever* recommend that a young person carry a knife or a gun. It is against the law. It is wrong. The crook's weapon, if there is one, is one too many. A weapon at school is like death looking for a place to happen. Some crime prevention authorities recommend small canisters of tear gas or pepper gas spray. We don't. There are several problems. The first is the law. In some states, the civilian use of spray is illegal. In most schools, you could be suspended or expelled for carrying a device like this. The second problem is that these devices are not all they are cracked up to be.

While police officers use them, "their" gas is three or four times more potent than the commercial stuff sold at your mall. The manufacturers of these materials do not tell you that tear gas and pepper spray have a shelf life. The spray deteriorates quickly when stored. The tear gas canister your mom has been carrying on her key ring for the past five years was "dead" or "inert" at least 3½ years ago. It has a probable shelf life of no more than 1½ years. If it was stored on a warehouse shelf for any length of time, it could have been useless the day she bought it. Also, the gas spray gives her a false sense of security. She thinks, "If I get in trouble, I will spray the robber or rapist with it."

What she ought to be doing and what you ought to be doing is avoiding the threat and avoiding the risk. You should be observing your environment and leaving the area if anything makes you feel uncomfortable. You should not say, "I will spray the sorry, contemptible, excuse of humanity with pepper spray. That will teach him." What you will probably do is just make him mad. Most of the gas and spray manufacturer advertising claims are misleading.

Some gas manufacturers claim that their product sprayed on a crook will "incapacitate him for 15 to 30 minutes." That is advertizing hype (hyperbole). Some people would say, "bull." Spray doesn't work that well. Ask almost any police officer about the times when he used it and it didn't work, and his is three or four times more powerful. If you do use a spray, buy the same stuff that police officers carry. Almost all large cities have a police supply store or two. Call your police department and get a telephone number or you can order what you need online.

Instead of a spray, use a portable alarm. Keep fresh batteries in it. Use an air horn or a good-quality police whistle. You can always use a power yell. Then run from your trouble. Depending on yourself, your observational skills, your running ability, and your power yell is much more useful than fishing around in your purse or backpack looking for a device that may not work the day you need it the most.

7
TRAVELING SAFELY

Charles and his sister, Kathy, live in an inner-city apartment, living only three blocks from their school. Because they reside in a high crime area, they must walk through two gang turfs, an illegal drug sales market, and a group of prostitutes every day. To say the least, they are apprehensive about their safety. Several of their friends have been mugged. Charles and Katie are always concerned and sometimes frightened. They are very careful every day.

They wear school clothes and carry book packs. They never stare at the creeps, MICAs (mentally incompetent and chemically addicted), or the prostitutes. Sometimes they walk past cars where these girls are selling sex. They never stare (nor should you), but they are aware of everything going on in their area.

If you live in a nice suburb and your school is right down the street, choosing your daily travel route may not be a major decision. However, if you live in the inner city or in a rough neighborhood, this may be your most important daily decision. Guys cruising for adventure, gang members, drug pushers, prostitutes, perverts, or kidnappers could be an everyday issue in your neighborhood, or in anybody's neighborhood. All of these security risks should be avoided whenever possible.

Many teens become victims because they are in the wrong place at the wrong time. Are you at that location because you must be? Do you have any alternatives or did you make a bad decision? Your daily route plan is very important. Sometimes you may avoid a trap by varying your route or the time of your entry or departure. These are actions you can easily control, so your decisions are important ones.

> Choosing your route to school may be the single most important security decision you will make each day.

> The best crime countermeasure a young person can take is to run. Some run and yell at the same time. A power yell can be heard for blocks.

Some threats are predictable. Others are spontaneous. A *predictable threat* is one that you know about. You should know where the gangsters, wannabees, prostitutes, or drug pushers hang out, so you try to avoid those locations. Walk by another route, even if this decision makes you walk farther. If you want to avoid looking like you are afraid, walk to the grocery store on an adjacent street. Get a candy bar or something. Do anything to justify walking another way. Do whatever it takes to keep your pocketbook, your dignity, and your safety.

A *spontaneous threat* is one that surprises you. You walk the same way you have for years and, all at once, you are confronted with a frightening event. Look out for MICAs. Perhaps it is a homeless person with mental problems, a drunk, somebody high on drugs, a gang member, or a rapist. Whatever the threat is, avoid it. Your avoidance plan didn't work today, so you must, as they say in the military, take countermeasures. The best countermeasure a young person can take is to run. You take countermeasures because you have been alerted. The most important difference between crime victims and nonvictims is that nonvictims stay poised and alert, ready to avoid high-risk threats.

A spontaneous threat is more likely to occur when you are alone, preoccupied with personal problems or tired. Students who are *under the influence of alcohol or drugs* are the most vulnerable of all. Fatigue, personal problems, alcohol, and drugs all serve to make you less attentive and help to confuse you. These factors also increase the chances of getting lost in a danger zone.

YOU ARE PSYCHOLOGICALLY VULNERABLE IF YOU ARE:

- Lost
- Inattentive
- Preoccupied

- Confused
- Tired
- Under influence of alcohol
- Under influence of drugs

Choose a Familiar Route

Always choose a familiar route. Check out alternative routes with family or friends if you are unfamiliar with adjacent territory. You should never risk getting lost in a hostile neighborhood. Getting lost accelerates psychological vulnerability. It increases the chances that you cannot influence the environment. It increases the risk that you might be surprised by an individual thief or even an entire gang. Being in unfamiliar territory also increases the risk that you will be isolated from your friends and your escape routes.

After deciding your route, you also must take charge of all other activities that influence your security. Let's say you are walking to school or to the bus stop. You must do two things simultaneously. First, you should walk in the middle of the sidewalk, unless there is a safety reason not to. This keeps you from being surprised by someone in an alleyway, a door, or in a car.

Always walk facing traffic. Cars will be coming toward you in this position. You can always see them. You also can see a threat from undesirable persons.

You should walk in the opposite direction of traffic. This means that cars are coming toward you. So, if a creep wants you to ride with him, get away from him by continuing to walk forward. He or she must back up, or go forward, make a u-turn, or traverse the block. Any of these activities are in your favor. If you walk with the flow of traffic, somebody can drive by, grab you from behind, and pull you into a panel van. If the van is soundproofed, nobody will even hear you scream.

> ## YOU ARE MORE VULNERABLE IF YOU ARE
>
> - Lost
> - Isolated
> - Immobilized
> - Accessible
> - There is no apparent escape route

When you walk facing traffic, you are protected from the drunk or the driver who just had a heart attack. By facing traffic, your ability to anticipate a risk and get out of the way is increased. If a car is coming from behind and there is no unusual noise to alert you, an out-of-control vehicle could easily turn you into fresh road kill.

There Are Always Alternatives

If you see a creep walking toward you, cross the street for a time, and then stay on the "safest side." The safe side changed when the MICA, gangbanger, or creep showed up on your side. If it is late and there isn't much traffic, you can walk in the street itself. This gives you a lot more room to maneuver if someone attacks. If it's an emergency, walk (or run) in the street even if the traffic is heavy. There may be less risk from traffic than from the thug who wants to attack you.

As you observe your environment carefully, you should avoid all blind spots and recessed doorways. As you walk near an alley entrance, listen for vehicles both in the street or in the alley. If it is safe to do so, you could even walk into the street in a semicircular pattern. Your destination, of course, is the sidewalk on the other side of the alley. Also avoid large shrubs, trees, and dumpsters. Give them a wide berth. Your intention is to remain safe, avoiding any unacceptable risk or surprise.

Try not to look directly into the sun. The best idea is to walk where you can observe others, not necessarily where they can easily observe you. This is a part of your avoidance plan, of learning avoidance techniques *before* your crime, so you are fully prepared. Most victims become victims because they are caught by surprise, don't know what to do, and are so terrified that they cannot think or respond. They lose by default. If you plan for the worst possible events, you will not lose by default.

Especially be careful when the street is deserted. Let's say that you see few pedestrians and very little traffic. If anyone asks for directions, listen to your feelings. If this person gives you the creeps or makes you suspicious, continue to walk on. Under these circumstances, it's not necessary for you to be polite to adults. In fact, you may be rude on occasion.

"Safety before courtesy" is a good rule. If you decide to help someone with directions, stand in the middle of the sidewalk and tell them how to get to their destination. Do not (and I mean *NEVER*) approach their car or lean over the window to give them this information. This is a good rule for all students of either sex. Keep the "distance" advantage and you will avoid their trap. If there is no trap, there is still no harm done.

If you feel that someone is stalking you, turn around. Turn all the way around. This motion is called a "6 o'clock" in the military services. A 180-degree turnaround allows the opportunity to fully see your potential assailant. Don't just look sideways or watch someone sideways with your peripheral vision. Gavin DeBecker, in the *Gift of Fear: Survival Signals that Protect Us from Violence*, says:

> It is better to turn completely, take in everything and look squarely at someone who concerns you. This not only gives *you information* but it *communicates to him* that you are not a tentative, frightened victim-in-waiting. You are an animal of nature, fully endowed with the hearing, sight, intellect, and dangerous defenses. *You are not easy prey, so don't act like you are.*[1]

YOU ARE SAFER IF YOU

- Walk with others
- Walk near the center of the sidewalk
- Stay away from hiding places

- Walk facing traffic
- Scan traffic and sidewalk both front and back
- Keep moving
- Walk erect
- Make eye contact with passersby
- Control your facial expressions
- Have a "neutral" expression
- Be careful when lending aid
- Keep cash out of sight
- Keep cash readily available
- Stay in well-lighted areas

Whenever someone asks for directions, change for a parking meter, or a light for his/her cigarette, listen to your instincts. Leave quickly if there is any bad feeling. Don't process these thoughts. Don't even think about it. Don't analyze the situation. Just leave. Hurting someone's feelings is preferable to being attacked or being hurt physically or emotionally.

In their book, *The 7 Steps to Personal Safety*, Tim Powers and Richard Isaacs said that "you need *distance*, about 12 feet or more in a public place. With friends, a polite distance is 4 to 12 feet."[2] Close friends usually grant a personal space of 2 to 4 feet. Intimates like boyfriends and girlfriends allow direct contact or close contact, say no more than 2 feet.

The average attacker can cover 5 feet in one quarter of a second, 10 feet in under three quarters of a second, and 21 feet in a second and a half.[3] This is not a lot of time to react, especially since most attackers seldom tip their hand until they are ready to strike. They act in a nonthreatening manner until the precise moment they attack.

THE SCIENCE OR STUDY OF MOTION AND DISTANCE

- Kinesics
- Proxemics

Watch the people walking toward you. Their motions are called kinesics. Reaching for a knife or making a fist is a threatening motion and falls within the study of kinesics. Proxemics relates to distance and the study of distance. Maintain a safe distance from others, especially those who may appear threatening. This is called "a *circle of safety.*" Some authorities refer to a cushion of space, a boundary, or a comfort zone. These terms are synonymous. This distance gives you time to react, time to maneuver, and time to respond. You will be much safer when you keep this rule.

Take Your Friends with You: Form Crime Avoidance Partnerships

Everybody needs a friend. You also need the right kinds of friends. Let's say that Johnny and Robert live nearby. They would be naturals for forming a protection pact. However, if Johnny sells or uses drugs or if Robert is the neighborhood bully, they both stand a strong chance of being attacked wherever they go. If you are with either of these boys, you may be attacked as well.

Pick some "good" friends to accompany you. The walk rules are the same when there are several young people involved. Insofar as possible, avoid gang turfs. You still should stay away from dumpsters and alleys, but there are some additional rules for females. If two or more girls are walking, they should put their purses to the inside. That is, the girl on the left should carry her purse to the right and the girl on the right should carry her purse to the left.

The purses should be touching or at least close. This placement deters both the mugger and the purse snatcher. The purse to the outside gives him direct access, a way to get to you and to get away from you, without knocking you or your friend down. When you carry to the "inside," he will have to assault you both to get one or both purses. He probably won't attempt this unless he thinks you have a big bankroll. Your purse flap should also be facing toward you, making it more difficult for a pickpocket. In cold weather, put your coat on over your purse, while it is already looped around your shoulder.

Boys and girls can do the same thing with their wallets. Put them to the inside, or carry your wallet in your jacket pocket or in a snug-fitting trouser front pocket. Many crime-conscious students sew Velcro®

in their pockets and on their wallets. Others place a pocket comb lengthwise across their wallet with the teeth pointed up. If someone attempts to pick your pocket or jerk your wallet out, the comb gets stuck. Inside your pocket, the comb is pretty strong, so it's not likely to break.

> You are always more vulnerable when you are alone.

Friends can help prevent crime, for each other and for themselves. You are always more vulnerable when you are alone. Being alone is the single factor most often associated with crime. If you are not alone, you are less vulnerable. One San Francisco crime study showed that walking with one other person reduces your chance of being a victim by 67 percent.[4] Two or more friends walking together lowers your chances of being victimized by 90 percent.[5] Go to school or the bus stop with your friends. Plan your routes ahead of time and travel together.

Even though you are lessening your likelihood of becoming a crime victim when you travel with your friends, you still should stay alert. There is an unusual group phenomenon known as *group paralysis*. Each group member is waiting for another group member to do something. When nobody moves, the collective response is to do nothing. The same thing happens to individuals, but psychologists call it *frozen fright* when applying it to an individual.

However, this doesn't need to happen to you. Because you are observing your environment, analyzing what you observe, and reacting to your observations, you may react more quickly than any of your friends. Exert leadership and direction here to your couch potato friends. Tell them what to do and set the example by doing it yourself. Nonvictims act to remove themselves from danger quickly. You decrease your chances of being a victim when you control your actions and reactions.

Using School and Public Restrooms

Johnny saw them and knew they didn't belong. They were too old to be fellow students, but instead of exiting quickly and using another restroom, he went in anyway. He obeyed the security rules by going into a stall and locking the door. However, as he exited, one big fellow grabbed him and pushed his face into a toilet. Struggling for breath, Johnny couldn't prevent his wallet being taken by a second guy. The third thief served as a door lookout.

Johnny made a serious judgment error when he decided to stay in the restroom. Had he returned quickly to the hallway, he would have been safer.

You would think that most restrooms are safe, but actually they are like magnets. Restrooms attract undesirables, thieves, perverts, and rapists. Public restrooms *inside* busy buildings are safer than the lonely, rarely used facility with an outside access door.

Service station restrooms with entrances from the outside are even more dangerous. Most modern service stations and fast-food restaurants have their restrooms on the inside. Usually, the inside restroom is safer. Outside restrooms should be avoided whenever possible. Should you have an "emergency," you can leave your friends outside while you go in. If several crime avoidance partners are with you, leave some outside and take the others in with you. This is another good example of "security partnerships."

When you open the door of any restroom, look around carefully to see if there are any threats. A large, busy restroom is safer. Creeps and thieves are less likely to bother you when others are there. Hold onto your possessions while you are in the restroom.

Boys, you are extremely vulnerable in a public restroom. Facing the urinal, your back is to the open area and to your assailant. In dangerous areas, you may prefer to use the private cubicles. Some boys always use the cubicle, even to the point of sitting to urinate, rather than turning their back on strangers. However, there is a moment of vulnerability as you are pulling your trousers up or down, so this is not always the best alternative. If your buddies are with you, take turns using the toilet or urinal. Both can watch for danger while the third is distracted.

Girls, do not put your purse on the floor when you sit on the toilet. Hold it in your lap or loop it over a clothing hook. If someone asks you for toilet paper or to return something they dropped, push it over with your foot and bring your foot back to the center of the toilet cubicle quickly. Do not *hand* the item to them. If they are thieves or perverts, they might grab your hand. You could be pulled off balance and onto the restroom floor before being attacked.

Bus or Subway Travel

Plan for bus or subway travel just as you would your walk to school. One of the best rules is to minimize your waiting time. If a bus comes by your favorite stop every 15 minutes on a reasonably precise schedule, then you could "time" your wait for just 3 or 4 minutes instead of 10 or 15. The bus stop is another *"magnet"* to thieves and rapists. As you wait, use the buddy rule. Wait with other people, preferably friends.

Keep crime avoidance partnerships intact. Each of you is safer because the other is there. It is really nice when an older teenager or adult can accompany you. They are often called guardians. Never assume, however, that adult strangers or others will come to your aid if or when you get in trouble. There are no guarantees. In criminal attacks, you may well be facing your perpetrator all alone, even though others are physically present. They may be immobilized, frightened, or perhaps will choose to mind their own business.

WAITING FOR THE BUS OR SUBWAY

- Wait with others.
- Minimize your wait.
- Stand away from the road/rail.
- Have bus fare or token ready.
- Be confident when boarding.
- See who is aboard.
- Sit near driver or operator.
- Sit where you can see.
- Sit near an aisle.
- Sit near an exit.
- Don't sit by anyone who seems out of place or who gives you the creeps.
- Stay away from MICAs.

Keep your bus fare or token handy. Don't let everyone around see how much cash you have. If you have planned for this each day, you just reach for your token or the correct change.

If you must buy a ticket or a token at a station and somebody creepy gets in behind you, deal with the problem quickly. You could turn around and ask them, "Are you going to buy a ticket?" I know that you would prefer not to talk to them at all, but this is the safest thing to do. If the answer is, "yes, I'm buying a ticket," then say "go on ahead of me, please, my bus/tram/subway doesn't leave for a while." You need to stand *behind* suspicious persons. Don't let them stand behind you. In some cities, particular tokens or tickets let the creep know where you are going. By letting him leave after he buys his ticket, you are depriving him of this information.

> Don't ride this particular bus or subway if anyone or anything gives you the creeps.

As you board, look at the passengers. If somebody left over from the latest psycho movie, or a gang, is riding, get off before you pay or drop your token in the receptacle. Don't sit near anyone that gives you the creeps or that you feel uneasy about. Sit as close to the driver as you can. *The nearer the driver, the safer you are.* Sit where you can see and sit near an exit. An aisle seat is safer than a window seat because you can't be blocked in by a creep. Girls are less likely to be "accidentally on purpose" pawed by some disgusting pervert.

> The nearer the driver, the safer you are.

Observe your stop carefully before you exit. If you see anything that bothers you, don't get off. Take the next safe exit or travel to the end of the line and get off on the way back. You can control your schedule even if someone is stalking you or if a predator is waiting. Most creeps won't wait that long.

Riding in a Taxi

Never take a "maverick" or unlicensed taxi. They may be cheaper, but they aren't regulated by the police or safety inspectors, so you are at a higher risk. Pick a distinctive cab with a well-known company. If possible, use the buddy system. Take someone else with you instead of traveling alone.

Never get in a cab with a stranger as a fellow passenger. An unknown driver and the unknown fare increases your risk. If someone else gets into the cab after you, get out quickly. You are paying for a ride by yourself, not a group rate.

Tell your driver where you are going and the fastest way to get there. If he takes another route, or gives you the creeps, get out at your next opportunity. If you have the cellular phone recommended previously, call and tell your mom what cab you are in (the number is usually posted on the dashboard) and when you plan to arrive. This call increases your safety. You can do this casually, not like you distrust your driver. Just say, "Hi Mom, I'm running late again. I am at _____ (give your approximate location) in cab _____ (give the taxi company name and the city cab license number posted on the dashboard). I'll be arriving in approximately _____ (give your approximate arrival time)."

One widely applied security method can be used at the pickup address. With the driver watching you, write down the number of the cab and give it to a friend who is not riding, or a friend who is riding in another cab. If there are two carloads of folks going in the same direction, both sets of cab occupants should exchange cab numbers. This is like an accounting audit; it helps keep everybody honest. Adults should do this, too. It helps keep all of these passengers safe from the perils of crime.

If You Drive

Your car can help you get away from trouble, but it can get you into serious difficulty as well. Your car can be an escape vehicle, but it also can be a trap. The car can be the target itself. Some automobile and truck models are more frequently hijacked than other models. Some guy walks up to you with a gun and takes your car away from you. Sometimes he takes you along. Most cars are hijacked between 10 p.m. and 2 a.m. when fewer people are around to intrude or to serve as guardians.

Get home before midnight and drive on well-traveled and well-lit roads. Avoid 24-hour, self-serve stores after dark. After-hour shopping increases the risk of hijacking, mugging, robbery, kidnapping, and rape, so fill your car's gas tank in the daytime. Buy your soda at the same time. Avoid car wash facilities and self-serve stores after daylight hours.

Here is how you can lessen your risk while in route. Let's say you are traveling down a four-lane street. The safest lane is the inside lane nearest the center of the street. Quite often drivers are attacked at intersections. Don't drive right up behind the car in front of you. Give yourself room to evade any attacker, so leave at least a car length between your car and the vehicle in front of you.

Let's say that you are stuck in traffic at a stoplight. If your car is two feet behind the car in front of you and someone else is up against your rear bumper, then you are stuck. However, if you left yourself room to maneuver and you are in the inside lane when the thief intrudes, you can still take off. You can get in the wrong lane, make a U-turn, drive past other cars against the light, or go up the street against the flow of traffic, blowing your horn and blinking your flashing emergency flashers all the way. Even if you must go slowly, you can still move. If you can't move your car, you are stuck and you are already a victim.

WHEN DRIVING

- Drive near the center of the street.
- At traffic lights, keep plenty of distance between your front bumper and the car in front of you.
- If someone bothers you, start honking, turn on your hazard lights, and call 911 on your cell phone.

If you keep the cellular phone with you at all times, you can use it now. If you don't have one, buy a realistic looking toy phone at the mall for two bucks and pretend to call. This may be sufficient to prevent an intrusion.

PARKING HINTS

- Park away from visual obstructions.
- Park away from vans.
- At night, park in well-lit areas.
- Avoid occupied vehicles.
- As a pedestrian, avoid cars in motion.
- As you walk to your car, look under it, and in the back seat before entering.
- Stay alert, your life depends on it.

Let's say you are driving to a school function at your local mall. Your favorite choral group is going to sing at a common-access area. What should you do to ensure your safety? First, you should park carefully. When you get to the mall parking lot, drive around it at least once. Watch for any threats to your safety. If there are any potential risks, move to another area of the mall parking lot or come back later. You don't have to park *this second*, do you? When you park, ensure that there are no visual obstructions. Make sure you can see any threat before you exit your car and before you reenter it. Wherever possible, back into your parking place. At night, park in a well-lighted area. Keep your car locked and make sure that your valuables are not exposed. Leave them in the trunk.

When you return to your car, try not to be overloaded. It is better to make multiple trips than to carry too much at once. You are more vulnerable when you are weighted down. As you exit the store for the parking lot, scan the parking area to make sure that there no threats exist. You may be tired, but you need to stay alert. Look out for moving vehicles. Stationary vehicles may be threats as well. Move over a lane if someone is driving near. As you approach your car, you should try to see under it. Recently, some thieves and rapists have hidden under the car. They grab their victim by the ankle and pull her down prior to robbery and/or rape. If you feel threatened or intimidated in any way, get a security officer to walk with you. They will be glad to help.

PARKING HINTS

- Park away from visual obstructions.
- Park away from vans.
- At night, park in well-lighted areas.
- Avoid occupied vehicles.
- As a pedestrian, avoid cars in motion.
- As you walk to your car, look under it.
- Stay alert, your life depends on it.

Looking under your car as you approach it, avoiding moving vehicles, walking around other vehicles, and avoiding vehicles that are occupied will increase your safety and lessen your risk. Also, you should be especially careful about vans. Stay away from them whenever possible. That side door and the darkened glass could be your trap … "said the spider to the fly."

Be wary if you discover a flat tire, especially if the tire is new and in good condition. Someone may have punctured it or removed your air-valve core. If your car won't start even though it was running perfectly when you parked, consider the possibility that someone has sabotaged it. Be especially wary of the nice stranger who suddenly appears out of nowhere and is interested in helping you. You should pick the person to help. Don't let a stranger pick you.

Riding Your Bike

Always take your bike lock with you. In most cities, the bike won't be there when you come back if it is not secured. While riding, you should always remember to wear your safety helmet. It will protect you from traffic accidents, but also from personal assaults as well. If someone attacks, duck your head and take the blow on the helmet. An incoming blow won't hurt you, but it sure will damage your attacker's fist.

You can always ditch the bike and run in a rural setting, but a mountain bike should take you anywhere: ditches, curbs, sidewalks, and maneuvers between parked cars. Don't drive fast near pedestrians and pay special attention to safety issues, but ride like the wind when threatened.

Ride with friends when you can, dependable riders, not local thugs or gangsters. Bad company will always get you into their fight. If gangsters try to cut you off, don't panic. Always be looking for alternate routes, even between houses, lots, and alleys. Just don't get trapped in a dead end.

References

1. DeBecker, G. 1997. *The gift of fear: Survival signals that protect us from violence.* New York: Little, Brown and Company, 69.
2. Powers, T., and R. B. Isaacs. 1993. *The seven steps to personal safety.* New York: Center for Personal Defense Studies, 27.
3. Ibid., 29.
4. Castleman, M. 1983. *Crime free: Stop your chances of being robed, raped, mugged or burglarized by 90%.* New York, Simon and Schuster, 67.
5. Ibid.

8

AVOIDING TROUBLEMAKERS

Some of the students at Cindy's high school could only be described as "really strange, young people." Since there hasn't been a large amount of violence there at Richville High, the principal has allowed students to "do their own thing." There are no color or clothing restrictions. The Richville mayor, Chamber of Commerce, and city manager all say that "Richville doesn't have troubles with youth gangs, drugs, and deviant cults." But, even though the police chief says the same thing, you question this statement because you see black lipstick and black nail polish on students dressed in black clothing holding *Satanic Bibles*.

You also know that several students are selling drugs on campus, and that one group of the student body has formed a group called the Outlaws. Rumor has it that an applicant must commit a theft or some other serious crime prior to being considered for membership. You saw the grip of a pistol sticking out of the Outlaws' vice president's belt yesterday.

The authorities tell you that everything is all right at your school, but your mind tells you that things do not look all right at all. You need to determine the "truth" about security at your school. How do you recognize those who might threaten your safety? More importantly, you need to learn how can you avoid them.

Who Are the Troublemakers?

Some troublemakers are easy to spot. They dress like troublemakers and they act like troublemakers. Others are as hard to spot as an undercover narcotic agent or a spy in the Central Intelligence Agency.

If you see a homeless woman coming toward you pushing a grocery cart filled with junk, you should take precautions. The same is true for a staggering drunk or someone strung out on drugs. One avoidance method would be to move to the opposite side of the walk. Another might be to cross the street. Still another might be to duck into a store or business, watching as they walk by. The MICAs (mentally incompetent, chemically addicted), the homeless woman, the drunk, and the street artist whose mind has been drug burned are all easily recognized.

These deviants are not authorized to be in your school; but there are several other "types" of potentially dangerous people, both students and nonstudents, who choose to frequent your school. They are visible because they wear "colors," bandannas, and jackets that identify them. Sometimes the color or even the angle a baseball cap is tilted signals that its wearer is a gang member. Your most visible school risk is the gang member. Members of violent gangs are "death looking for a place to happen." There are, however, other "less visible" potential troublemakers.

Bullies

Many teenagers are afraid of particular bullies. Virtually every classroom and every school is affected by bullying. Over 800,000 students nationwide skip school each day because they are afraid to go.[1] One out of every 12 students who quits school at an early age stops going because he or she is afraid to go.[2] These students are literally pushed out of school. They don't "drop out" for traditional academic failure or economic reasons; they abandon their studies because they are scared to death. Some of the students who are frequently absent are skipping school because they are afraid, not because they are delinquent. Bullying victims are left with psychological scars that last years after the intimidation stops.

According to the 2000 Census and the Norwegian Study of Dr. Dan Olweus and Brenda High, founder of the Bully Police USA, there were an estimated 8,824,833 school-age children involved in bullying. This included both victims and bullies. It has been reported as being approximately 1 percent, but the Bully Police Study estimated the amount of bullying to be more than 16 percent.[3]

Tammy Quarles, school counselor and co-author of this book, believes this figure to be underestimated, that a larger percentage of students are being bullied today. Many students are intimidated in small ways and do not report the event. Bullying does not always involve being pushed around, beaten, raped, or robbed. A student can be bullied by being teased, gossiped about, or "left out" of the "in crowd."

And now many children are being victimized by the *cyberbully*, the newest application of abuse. Our technology, casual access to cell phones and the Internet, gives the cyberbully an opportunity to victimize young people through text messaging, e-mail, instant messaging, chat rooms, Web pages, and other forms of communication used to harass and harm others. Victimization occurs through spreading gossip, making threats, sending altered or private information, or in placing a person's facial photo over a nude or altered Internet photo designed to embarrass or humiliate.[4]

Cyberbullies victimize their targets at school, at home, day or night, becoming an ever-present threat. The young person doesn't feel safe at school, at home, or anywhere. And, the cyberbully remains anonymous. In *A Parent's Guide to Cyberbulling and Cyberthreats*, the author had these recommendations for cyberbully victims.[5]

1. DO NOT RESPOND to text messages or Internet messages.
2. DO NOT ERASE THE MESSAGES OR PICTURES. Print and save them for evidence.
3. BLOCK THAT PERSON'S NUMBER< EMAIL< CODE NAME<WEB SITE from you computer.
4. TELL YOUR PARENTS, SCHOOL COUNSELOR, OR ANOTHER ADULT YOU TRUST.
5. HAVE THE ADULT HELP YOU CONTACT THE INTERNET PROVIDER OR PHONE COMPANY TO REPORT INAPPROPRIATE USE OF THEIR SERVICE AND TO HELP IDENTIFY THE BULLY.
6. HAVE AN ADULT HELP YOU CONTACT THE POLICE IF THE CYBERBULLYING INVOLVES:
   a. Threats of violence
   b. Extortion (demands for money or valuables)
   c. Obscene or harassing phone calls or text messages
   d. Harassment, stalking, or hate crimes
   e. Pornography

The percentage of schoolchildren being bullied has been grossly underestimated in many media publications. Male bullies are usually *larger* than their victims. One rather unusual statistic reveals that female bullies are usually *smaller* than the students they pick on. They simply use the power of their strong personalities and are willing to use force to intimidate less aggressive students. Both male and female bullies feel a need to use force, intimidation, and to control the behavior of others.

They also are sadistic; that is, they like to hurt and embarrass others. Sadism is a deviancy in which the bully gets pleasure out of scaring, intimidating, or hurting another person. Most bullies enjoy administering abuse, but abusing others also causes problems for the bullies. Sometimes the kid he abused for years outgrows the bully and seeks revenge. At any rate, the violence spirals wherever bullies operate.[6]

Bullies are a problem that all students must encounter. Helping bullies learn how to handle conflict is an important effort because a large percentage of all bullies go to prison. Bullies can usually be spotted by their eighth year. The more aggressive 8-year-old is very likely to come into frequent police contact as a teenager and an adult. Aggressive boys are less likely to finish college or to obtain good jobs. Aggressive girls grow up to be the mothers of bullies.

Unfortunately, a bully is often seen as "cool." They feel powerful because they can harass, harm, or insult others. When we think about a bully, we often visualize an image of a big, overbearing boy, although there are many girls who are bullies as well. According to research conducted by the Girls Scout Research Institute and Harris Interactive, Inc.,[7] girls are more often emotional bullies, spreading harmful gossip about their victims and forming cliques that exclude their victims. Sometimes girls respond to the gossip and feelings of being an outsider to the popular crowd by seeking negative attention and engaging in risky behavior, such as the use of alcohol, drugs, or sexual behavior.[7] Girls are about twice as likely as boys to be the cyberbully and also to be the cyberbully victim.[5]

If you have been bullied, please get adult help. At least make an appointment with your school counselor. Bullying increases the number of days kids skip school and some teens literally get sick, their grades start falling, and they get clinically depressed, even to the point of considering suicide or of returning to school to kill their tormenter.

If bullies can learn how to resolve conflict and not push people around, they may avoid this penalty. If they can learn not to menace, they might even be able to compete and succeed in our society. If they don't learn this lesson, they will not succeed. In fact, bullies are *three times* more likely to be jailed than their friends. In the meantime, they are harming others.

TROUBLEMAKERS

- Bullies
- Truants and tardy students
- Weapon carriers
- Gang members
- Drug traffickers and substance abusers
- Ritualistic groups
- Vigilantes

Truants and Tardy Students

Unhappy or academically marginal students are often called dysfunctional by the education community. These are the students who cause over 90 percent of all school problems. According to Professor James Q. Wilson of UCLA,[8] 5 to 6 percent of the teenagers and young boys commit half or more of all serious crimes, so the troublemakers should be watched.

Students who skip class frequently are normally the biggest troublemakers at school. Frequent absenteeism and tardiness is one major "troublemaker" predictor. Statistics indicate that students who miss between 5 to 50 class periods each year commit most of the serious school offenses.[9] High school freshman and sophomore students tend to commit more offenses, as do those students with lower grade point averages. Males commit more offenses than females. Beware of these potential troublemakers.

Weapon Carriers

A small percentage of students today are carrying weapons to school. While fewer guns are seized by police than other types of weapons, we are seeing a significant increase in gun-related school crimes. At school, any weapon is a significant threat to your well-being. Brass or aluminum "knuckles," knives (including fiberglass knives that will pass through metal detector scrutiny), blackjacks, razors, box cutters, and chemical irritants are all examples of school weapons.

Students carry weapons for a variety of reasons. Some think it gives them a mystique or some macho status. Others intend to steal, rob, or rape using the weapon for intimidation. Others are good students who are tired of being pushed around and don't want to be intimidated again. They don't want to use their weapon, but they choose not to be the only one without a weapon.

The firearm is the most lethal of all weapons. You are much more likely to survive a stabbing than a gunshot wound, but all weapons are potentially deadly. Please keep weapons out of your school. Keeping weapons, drugs, and alcohol out of your school is vital to your security.

Gang Members

Schools were once believed to be a "neutral" zone, relatively immune from gang violence. Now, schools are frequently used as recruiting stations and turf war battlegrounds. Let's create a fictitious group. We will call this gang the CGG (the Covenant Garden Gang), named after a gang from a local apartment complex. Gang members associated with this group may now claim that "the CGG is in charge of this school." Gangs cause a higher school dropout rate. They frequently rob students, taking their lunch and bus money. Other students are often coerced into joining the gang or suffer the consequences of frequent fights and intimidation.

Being in the presence of a gang member increases your risk of violence. You are not as safe as you could be just because the gang member is there. If an opposing gang member sees you with them, you could easily experience a "drive-by" shooting. Even a fistfight may have more serious consequences for onlookers because of the extreme violence.

Gang members are usually recruited between the ages of 11 and 15. Some street gangs recruit boys between the ages of 8 and 12. Gang members begin to gain strength and confidence while they are still in middle school or junior high. They stay in the gang until their twenties. Sometimes they can't leave. Too sudden a departure may be construed as betrayal. Gang peers may believe those departing have become police informants or that they have flipped (surreptitiously joined another gang). Sometimes gang members never leave, retaining lifetime membership. School officials unaware of the gang problem often tolerate their presence, never realizing that today's gangs are an organized criminal effort.

Contrary to popular belief, gangs are not restricted to minorities or to kids from disadvantaged neighborhoods. Gang members represent all racial and ethnic groups. Many middle-class and upper-class youth also are involved in gang activity.

Gang members like to strut. They are looking for attention. They appear menacing and increase the menace with sheer numbers, preferring to walk in groups of no less than 3, but usually with 5 to 10 clearly distinguishable members. Some call it a gang "shuffle." Their numbers, in or out of school, are intimidating. Sometimes the larger gangs are referred to as "wolf packs." It's an appropriate description.

Dr. Ronald Stevens, director of the National School Safety Center, says that "today's gangs pose a greater threat than at any time in recent history."[10] Gangs are presently within the boundaries of virtually *every* school district in the United States. Gangs are no longer just a boys' or girls' social club. Many gangs are formed for protecting their membership. Other gangs are formed exclusively for profit through criminal activity. Their primary crime is usually drug sales or drug "control" in your neighborhood.

In other cases, gangs extort (take by force, intimidate, or frighten children and young people into giving them *protection* money). For the privilege of using the restroom, a hallway, a sidewalk, or the cafeteria the unmolested young person must pay a "permission" tax. Young children and loners are extorted most often. The kids who don't pay are harassed, abused, and attacked. Older and larger students are usually left alone.

There have always been nonstandard lifestyles. Long hair, sideburns, ducktails (like Elvis), mustaches, boys' earrings, tattoos, and clothing styles were issues in the past. Today the primary issue is the gang itself, but gang colors, gang caps (the way the caps are worn), gang jackets, graffiti, signing (gang sign language), and drugs are the alternate issues. Sometimes gangs wear the jackets of particular professional sports teams as well as team caps or shirts. This was first done to help them "blend in" at school and in the street, but the symbolism is the same—it often means *gang*.

Pro-league jackets can become dangerous, as well. Joe Lee is not very observant. He also has the same favorite team as the local Gangster Disciples or the Urban Thugs. When Joe wears his new jacket to school, four things could happen. First, he could be associated with the gang. If there is to be a "rumble," he could easily be caught up in it. Second, the gang may be angry that he is wearing *their jacket* when he is not a member. Third, a Gangster Disciple is much more likely to steal Joe Lee's jacket. Fourth, an opposing gang may single Joe out for retribution over some past event believing him to be a member of the other gang.

Sometimes a community or a school can experience so much violence that young people join opposing gangs just to get the protection of gang membership. These prospective members want protection and influence. Gang power and influence is called "juice" in the gang community.

Many, if not most, gang members come from dysfunctional homes. The gang becomes a substitute support group instead of the traditional family. The gang offers friendship, self-esteem, status, rank, and money. Never forget that these guys use some forms of crime to *profit* from their gang association. Financial gain continues to be a powerful motive for gang involvement, especially in impoverished neighborhoods. Middle-class kids, however, need more money if they are doing drugs. Even rich kids overspend and may join for the cash.

At the extreme, however, the gang creates servitude. Gang members do what the gang bosses say to do. You keep their schedules, not yours. Some gangs do not and will not let you quit. You can't resign or retire. In some urban neighborhoods, three and four generations of a gang live in a single household. Often, the only way "out" of the gang is death. Because of this danger, gangs should always be prohibited, especially at school.

WHAT CAN YOU DO?

- Display friendly attitudes toward other students and teachers.
- Dress for success. Clean, inexpensive clothes, inexpensive jewelry, avoid gang colors.

- Students should not wear hair styles identifying themselves as gang members.
- Students should not wear gang colors.
- Students should not wear gang jewelry.
- Students should not wear gang tattoos or brands.
- Students should not use gang signals.
- Do not allow gang graffiti at your school. Students go to school. Gang members can associate elsewhere.

If your school doesn't have these rules now, you should ask your student government to pass them as formal policy and request that your school administration or school board accept them as well.

Gang Graffiti   Graffiti is one form of gang art. It communicates that a gang claims a particular territory. If someone paints gang symbols on a school wall, the artwork should be removed that same day.

Gang symbols and artwork should be removed quickly. The symbols establish a gang territory. Paintbrushes and paint should always be available. Students who have misbehaved or were tardy should be made to stay after school to paint over the graffiti each day.

If a student is caught spray painting or wall drawing, the school should require him to clean all of the graffiti for the next month or so. Repeat offenders should be turned over to the police for arrest and prosecution.

Some schools have Campus Pride campaigns. Student graffiti artists, wall drawers, and wall poets are challenged to compete in the design of acceptable slogans and posters used to encourage a positive atmosphere. The best artwork, both in drawings, painting, or spray art, is given awards and ribbons. The campus poets are rewarded as well and their work is published in the school student newspaper and in the school annual.

Keeping a school clean will make it safer. Gangs use the graffiti to establish "no trespassing" areas on their own turfs. If they ever establish control, then all nonmembers are at risk, even teachers and school staff. Removing the graffiti denies them "their" space and opens the areas for the use of everyone.

If your school staff is still in denial, that is, they still do not believe that gangs operate at your school, you may be the one who alerts them to the fact that there is a real problem. Denial, camouflaging, and downplaying are standard administrative reactions to gang problems. "We don't have gang problems at our school" is a typical denial reaction, especially when the gangs are clearly in evidence. With this administrative approach, the gangs are getting ever stronger while school administrators look the other way. Conscientious students must alert parents and school authorities. Let them know that there *is* a problem.

Substance Abusers

The Federal Office of Juvenile Justice Delinquency Prevention Research, Washington, D.C., claims that the proportion of students claiming to be high on drugs or under the influence of alcohol ranges from 2.2 percent at some schools to nearly 10 percent at others.[11] The number of students using recreational drugs is increasing all over America. At least 3 million teenagers are problem drinkers. The National Institute of Education's study on *Violent Schools—Safe Schools* reports that at least one in four of all high school students consume alcohol on a weekly basis and over 6 percent consume it every day.[12]

Many students seem to believe the myth that drug abuse is a "victimless crime." They believe that the teenagers abusing drugs and alcohol are only hurting themselves. This is not true. Nothing could be *further* from the truth. Drug crimes hurt the students who abuse them and they harm the students who come in contact with the abusers. The hallucinogenic chemicals (THC levels) in marijuana have been increasing over the past three decades, so this drug is more dangerous today than previously.

The frequent abuser is not learning at the same level as other students. Even really bright students who abuse drugs are decreasing the possibility of athletic or academic scholarships and college enrollment.

When students use cocaine, crack, methamphetamine, and halluci-nogenic drugs, they are gambling on their future. Usually they are gambling to lose.

DRUG-FREE SCHOOLS

Keep your school drug free. If the drugs are there, the money is there, and the weapons are there to protect the drugs, the money, and the pushers.

Drugs and drug pushers at school are a real safety and security prob-lem as well. There are several good reasons for this. It takes money to buy drugs, so there are increasingly larger sums at drug sale locations. The drug pusher often feels he must carry a weapon, either a knife or a gun, to keep his money. If he or she doesn't, that dealer will be robbed. Where there are drugs, there are rip-offs. Where there are rip-offs, there is vio-lence. Weapons, gangs, and violence proliferate in drug environments.

Keeping drugs and the gangs running or controlling the drug dis-tribution network out of middle schools and high schools may be the single most important security measure available. No other safe-school strategy will work as well. It then becomes very important for students to become involved in working for a drug-free school environment.

SAFE SCHOOLS

Ensuring that your school is drug free is the most important thing you can do for increased safety and security.

Ritualistic Groups

The United States Constitution separates church and state activities while guaranteeing religious liberty. In recent years, our govern-ment has chosen to separate religious activities from the classroom. Therefore, school authorities and students themselves should not tol-erate satanic cults operating in the school environment. This isn't a "cute" little social club. This isn't a group of students just showing their independence and variance with societal norms. It isn't "just" another religion. These teenagers believe in death, in ritualistic suicide, and sometimes in sacrificing a human "offering" to Satan. Usually these offerings are very young children, or even a member of their own group.

RITUALISM BELIEFS

Ritualistic groups believe in death, in ritualistic suicide, and in human sacrifice.

Sometimes the weirdos of your school are attracted to ritualistic groups because they don't connect with other students. Just like a gang, the ritualists offer status, group security, and a feeling of belonging. Students who are unhappy at home, school, and your community are especially likely to be recruited.

Satanists also use graffiti. If you don't know what to look for, you will miss it completely. You might even think it is just another form of "street art" or gang graffiti. Don't be deceived, however. It is not the same. Once you understand how the satanic artists operate, you may be able to interpret things you didn't before. Most graffiti artists put their artwork in prominent eye-level locations and satanists may do the same. However, the satanist also may create his/her artwork in the lowest possible location on a wall. If you say, "Goodness, the artist had to lie down on a dirty floor or in the mud to draw that," you may be looking at satanic artwork. The reason these artists draw their artwork as close to the ground or floor as possible is that they want it to be closer to Hell and to Satan. Lower placement allows this, according to their beliefs. The numbers *666* are the centuries-old symbols of Satan worship. These numbers are probably the most frequently used ritualistic symbols.

Ritualistic violence often includes human sacrifice as well as "serial" suicide. When this happens, several teenagers commit suicide within a few days of each other. Ritualists believe in a form of reincarnation. They commit suicide because they believe that they are taken to a better or higher life whenever they die. When police begin to find burned out candles in local cemeteries or a decapitated teenager, you can be sure that you are experiencing ritualism in your community. Some even have prefrontal lobotomies (a surgical procedure removing the brain's frontal lobe) in which they kill the victim in a formal ceremony, cut open her skull (it's a female, more often than not), and offer the brain to Satan.

If you have an unusual or bizarre suicide at your school, the probability is that you will have several more. *Cooperate with the police.* Tell the authorities who are the friends of the deceased. You may well save a life.

Vigilantes

YOUR MOST DANGEROUS STUDENT

In all probability, it is the vigilante who is the most dangerous student at your school. The vigilante is usually a good student—just like you.

Vigilantes are a way of life in America. When the authorities aren't protecting society, local people step in and do it themselves. Many movies and TV shows depict the strong individual seeking revenge when the justice organizations fail to act. These concepts are reinforced through our songs, rap music, movies, and TV shows. Violence is a part of our culture and that culture is reflected at school. Probably the vigilante is the most dangerous student at your school. If you are angry about the violence at your school, you too could easily become a vigilante. Don't use violence, however. Use parents, teachers, counselors, and law enforcement officers to help solve the problems at your school.

Picture this scenario. David and Suzy are always being pushed around by the gangs or the school bully. They have been embarrassed, intimidated, stolen from, and harmed. David has been extorted. Gang creeps took his lunch money. Once a gangster disciple even took the watch Johnny's dad gave him for his birthday. Suzy has been frequently harassed with harmful words. Billy, the bully, once leered at her and he put his hand down her blouse and into her bra with his friends looking on. They all laughed and thought he was "cool." Suzy was mortified, embarrassed, and ashamed. She still has nightmares about the incident.

David and Suzy are just the types of students to rebel. Johnny wants to get his watch back with his uncle's gun as an "equalizer." Suzy hid a butcher knife in a hollowed out section of an old textbook. She plans to slash the next guy who paws her. David and Suzy are drawing a line in the sand. The next time they are assaulted (physically or verbally), somebody is going to be hurt.

In Boston several years ago, there was a school rebellion. Several kids left school in an ambulance. The insurrectionists were probably the nicest kids at that school. They were tired of being abused, ripped off, and bullied. The girls were tired of being groped. They were tired of getting caught in the middle of gang conflict. They were tired of the campus drug pushers. They were tired of being scared and taking a lot of bull every day.

Their rebellion was spontaneous, overwhelming, and violent. Several drug pushers, bullies, and thugs were sent to the hospital in an ambulance. Even school officials and teachers were injured. This wasn't "just a fight," it was a rebellion. School was canceled for an entire week. School administrators went into crisis management sessions trying to figure out what had happened. They learned that the students did not believe the adult guardians had done a good job of maintaining order and they decided to do it themselves. They became vigilantes and took matters into their own hands. The students knew the school was not safe and were angry at teachers and administrators for their negligence. These teenagers were tired of being afraid.

This is why you need to learn conflict resolution skills. You need to know how to appropriately influence inappropriate conduct. You need to learn how before you explode in a violent rage. Kids who continue to be abused and bullied eventually rebel. When they do, it will be with an equalizer like a knife, a gun, or a baseball bat. When they rebel, everyone will be in danger, not just the rebels and their victims.

> When vigilantes rebel, everyone will be in danger.

When we don't keep our schools safe, we create vigilantes who become criminals because of their reactive violence. We encourage vigilantism because teenagers believe there is no other alternative when adult guardians have failed to keep the school safe. Teachers cannot compensate for these tensions.

When you help the school staff ensure that your school is a crime-free zone, that bullying is not tolerated, that the school is drug free, that student-age drug pushers must sell elsewhere during after-school hours, that the ritualists don't meet on school property, and that your school is gun free, there will be no reason for vigilantism. All will be safer because students are cooperating to create a secure environment.

References

1. Landen, W. 1992. Violence and our schools: What can we do? *Updating School Board Policies*, National Association of School Boards, 23 (1): 1–5.
2. Greenbaum, S., B. Turner, and R. D. Stephens. 1989. *Set straight on bullies*. Malibu, CA: The National School Safety Center, 9.
3. High, B. L. How many children are bullied in the USA? http://www.bullypoliceorg/BullyingNumbers.pdf
4. U.S. Department of Human Services. *Stop bullying now, take a stand, lend a hand, cyberbullying, what adults can do?* http://www.stopbullyingnow. hrsa.gov/indexAdult.asp?Area=cyberbullying
5. Willard, N. 2005. *A parent's guide to cyberbullying and cyberthreats*. Eugene, OR: Center for Safe and Responsible Internet Use.
6. Kids Health–For Kids. *Dealing with bullies*. Jacksonville, FL: Nemours Foundation. http://kidshealth.org/kid/feeling/emotion/bullies.html
7. Feeling safe: What girls say. *Pennsylvania State News*, Girl Scout Research Institute (www. gssp.org) in Conjunction with Harris Interactive, Inc. http://www.bullypolice.org/pa_girl_scouts.html
8. National Institute of Education. 1978. *Violent schools — safe schools: The safe school study report to the Congress*. Washington, DC: Superintendent of Documents, 92.
9. Cuervo, A. G., J. Lees, and R. Racey. 1984. *Towards better and safer schools*. Alexandria, VA: National School Board Association.
10. National School Center. 1999. *Gangs in schools: Breaking up is hard to do*. Oak Park, CA, 3.
11. Federal Interagency Forum on Child and Family Statistics. 1999. *America's children: Key national indicators of well-being*. Federal Interagency Forum on Child and Family Statistics, Washington, DC: U.S. Government Printing Office.
12. National Institute of Education, 14.

9

BECOMING A SUCCESSFUL VICTIM

Mike made the highest college entrance exam score in his city. He was invited to appear on a TV show honoring local scholars. Dressed up in his best clothes and wearing a tie and sport jacket, he headed downtown on the Z subway. Getting off at the correct stop, he walked right into trouble.

A bunch of guys wearing gangster clothes told him that he had to pay them for the privilege of walking through "their" territory. Mike told them he didn't have anything, but they didn't believe him. Grabbing him from behind, they took his wallet and even his return token. Afraid that a subway police officer would come in on the next car, they ran off, leaving Mike shaken, disheveled, and broke, without the means to return home.

It is easy to feel sorry for Mike because he was assaulted, intimidated, and robbed. Don't feel too sorry for him, however, because Mike is a "successful victim." He didn't go to the hospital and the coroner's hearse isn't taking him to the morgue in a body bag. He isn't a loser, he is a winner because he is still alive. If he had lost his temper, become hysterical, or started fighting against overwhelming force, he most certainly would have been seriously injured or killed. Let's examine the concept of the "successful" victim. We can do this by studying winners and looking at losers.

Winners and Losers

Just as there are winners and losers in life, there are also winners and losers in crime prevention. There are those who are successful. Some are never victimized. There are partial losers. Others keep their money or at least their lives. Those who fail in crime prevention lose their money and valuables. Sometimes they travel by ambulance to a hospital or in a hearse to the morgue.

Now don't misunderstand. All criminals are losers. Most look like losers. They talk like losers. They dress like losers. Crooks and creeps will never "really" win. Horribly enough, they also lose in their quest for happiness. Maybe some delinquents have avoided law enforcement investigation in the past, but someday they won't. Criminals can expect to spend a large portion of their lives behind bars.

Winners are successful victims. Some successful victims avoid the crime entirely. Jimmy saw the Cock-Roach Garden Gang approaching and altered his route home. He wasn't even intimidated, much less attacked. Shirley saw a creepy guy following her. Today, as she walked past the police officer directing traffic near her school, she told him that this stranger had been stalking her for several days. The officer investigated and the stalker never followed her again.

Sometimes you can be a winner by just surviving. Let's say that you are always as alert as a soldier in a war zone. You avoid crime and criminals. You don't wear expensive clothes or costly valuables. You never carry more money than you need to meet daily expenses. Many teenagers become victims just because they are in the wrong place at the wrong time. Sometimes this can be avoided. Sometimes it can't.

One day, two armed guys jump out of a van and rob you. How can you be successful when you have been robbed? This is a good question, a practical question, but there is a good answer. You can be successful by leaving, living, and surviving. You can be successful by avoiding the hospital or the morgue. The successful victim always survives.

SUCCESSFUL VICTIMS

- Leave
- Live
- Survive
- Avoid the hospital
- Avoid the morgue

What to Do during a Robbery?

Someone puts a knife in your ribs and wants your allowance. He wants it right now. You better let him have it. Sometimes the robber is a girl, but she has a knife, a box cutter, sharp scissors, or a gun. It's probably better to let her have your allowance. The time to stop this crime occurred before she attacked. The time to stop the crime occurred when you were supposed to be observant—and you weren't. Now it's too late. You let them get too close.

> The best advice during a robbery is to stay cool.

The best advice in a robbery is to stay cool. Don't overreact. Don't get hysterical. If you get excited, he will too. An excited robber is even more dangerous, so a hysterical reaction can easily get you killed. Whatever you do, don't scream or yell when the person with the knife is close enough to stab. Don't fight or resist when the threat of death or harm is immediate. If you can get away, do it quickly. "Flight before fight if at all possible" is a very reasonable crime avoidance approach in any street attack.

Otherwise, do what the robber tells you. Comply with his wishes. Be courteous. This sounds offensive to an assertive teenager, but respect and courtesy during a robbery can save your life. This is not the occasion to tell them what you think of thieves or to resist verbally in any way. Verbal or passive resistance can get you killed. Telling a robber that he is a thief or that he is evil is a quick route to the morgue. A young offender usually has a hostile response to *dis* (disrespect) and is willing to kill to guarantee respect for himself and his perceived status as a bad dude gangster.

While your chance of being murdered is only about 2 out of every reported 1,000 armed robberies, you must also remember that over 9 percent of all murder victims are killed during robberies. J. Edgar Hoover, the former director of the Federal Bureau of Investigation, once said that an armed robbery was "like death looking for a place to happen." He knew what he was talking about. Tread lightly. Don't take unnecessary risks with your life.

Be careful. Speak distinctly and appropriately. Don't make any sudden moves, but don't move too slowly either. If "your" crook thinks you are passively resisting by being too slow to respond to his demands, he may explode into a rage. Victims who act too quickly are also likely to be harmed. Any resistance encourages assault, injury, and murder.

Most robbers in America are young. Most are 19 years old or even younger, as are a disproportionate percentage of all their robbery victims. The bandits are young people stealing from other young people. An inexperienced or immature robber is much more dangerous than an experienced robber and is much more likely to use lethal force.

If you're looking down the barrel of a mean-looking pistol or are watching light reflect off the point of a dagger, *stop*. Start looking at your attacker. Look in his eyes. The pistol won't go off unless he pulls the trigger. If he slashes you, his facial features and body language will probably reflect his intentions. Speak quietly and with respect. Let him know everything is okay. You will let him have your watch, money, or ring. This is especially important when your robber or attacker is high or obviously under the influence of alcohol.

TIPS WHEN FACED WITH A ROBBERY

- Do exactly as the robber commands.
- Don't make any sudden movements.
- Do not speak unless you are ordered to.
- Don't risk your life for your money or other valuables.
- If a robber orders you to lie down, do so.
- Resist only if you believe he intends to kill you.
- Do not attempt to follow the robber.
- Call the police after the robber leaves.

Do exactly as the robber commands. Don't do anything he doesn't tell you to do. If he says to raise your hands, then do so, carefully. If he doesn't order you to put your hands above your head, then don't assume that these are his wishes. Do not speak unless you are ordered to do so. Nobody likes a smart mouth, especially a robber. Do not argue. Do not debate. Do not tell him how wrong he is or that robbery is an evil crime. If the robber orders you to lie down, then do so.

If he says to lie there for 10 minutes, this is okay, too. As long as he is leaving, this is an acceptable compliance.

Whatever you do, do not follow the robber. Just let him leave. He is just as dangerous upon leaving as he was pointing his weapon at you. If he or she senses pursuit, he may shoot. While police officers would like to discover where your robber lives or what make of car was used in the getaway, this is an incredibly dangerous activity. When the crime is over, call the police. If it is at school, tell the principal *after* you have called the police.

Sometimes the school administration resists the police response. In fact, one decade-old study revealed that over two thirds of all violent crimes *resulting in hospitalization* were not reported to the police by school authorities.[1] Another national study showed that two thirds of all school robberies are not reported to the police.[2] In the National Institute of Education study, several years ago, it was determined that "only one school crime in 58 is reported to the police."[3] Do not let the principal decide whether the police will be called when a serious crime has been committed. It's your decision alone, or yours and your parents, not the principal's.

If you are attacked, your primary concern should be to safely escape to a more secure location. In fact, you have very few choices if you are attacked with a weapon. You can run, resist, or comply. You can always resist if compliance is not separating you from danger. Resistance, however, should be the very last option considered. If you resist at first, it may be more difficult to change to a nonviolent compliance strategy later.

If you do choose to fight immediately, remember that you have several disadvantages. The first is that your assailant picked the location of this robbery. You are on his turf, his terms, and his schedule. He has many advantages and you have very few—perhaps none at all. If you choose to fight, fight to escape, not to win. As soon as you have attacked, run and evade. If you are still alive at the end of a fight, you are a "winner."

Whether you resist or whether you comply, you must prepare yourself immediately for escape. Stay calm. Focus your attention on your attacker. Agree to do what he wants. Tell him that you will cooperate. Watch him, not his weapon. Keep your confidence up. If he says he has a weapon, ask to see it. He may be bluffing. Be willing to give up your property if he does have a weapon.

Your property is not worth your life. Your possessions and cash are not worth an extended visit to the hospital. Separate yourself from your possessions. Give them to him. Better yet, drop them and run. If your attacker wants the money or the property more than he wants you, he will be diverted while you escape.

As long as you are talking, you are not being shot at or stabbed, so be willing to negotiate. By negotiate, I mean to discuss the crime. *Never plead or cry.* This gives the offender more power over you. Observe his behavior while you are talking to him. See if you can distract him. If not, give up your property.

DURING A ROBBERY OR SEXUAL ASSAULT

- Negotiate.
- Never plead or cry.
- Observe his behavior.
- Distract him.
- Never believe what he says.
- He is a liar.

Whatever you do, don't believe anything your assailant says. He is a criminal and a liar. He will tell you anything to get you to do what he wants. If you are a female, he might tell you to give up your money and to take off your clothes so you can't follow him while he escapes. He might even tell you that he won't hurt you or that he won't rape you. Don't believe him, no matter what he says. If you are going to resist, now is the time. Don't let him get any more control over you than he already has. Taking your clothes off will give him more power and lessen your options.

Now is the time to fight and escape, or submit. You are the only one who knows your capability or whether you have the emotional or physical stamina to resist. Listen to your instincts, develop your avoidance skills, and cope as well as you can.

> Don't get in an assailant's car—ever.

If the robber wants you to get into his car, this is the time to say no. Don't do it if you can prevent it, even if the perpetrator is threatening you with a gun. Run in the opposite direction. Run away from the direction his car is headed. A girl's chance of being raped or murdered increases considerably when she gets into the car. Her chances of being raped or killed on the street are fairly low. Even when a criminal has a gun, he may not want to use it. Gunfire, screams, or any other loud noise will attract attention. He doesn't want attention.

Some high crime neighborhood residents use additional protection measures. Girls may throw their purses and run. Boys or girls may have a "flash roll." This is called *appeasement money*. Many victims use an appeasement roll to "buy their way out of trouble." The roll includes several $1 bills rolled up inside a $5. If a crack head really wants your money, he will go after the cash while you escape. Some victims even say, "You can have the money. It's all I have." You are not going to be attacked ordinarily, though occasionally offenders are angry that they you didn't have as much money as they predicted. Many street robbers will just take the money and leave. A girl may throw her purse away. While he is distracted and moves to pick it up, she escapes.

Talk to your parents, teachers, and school counselors about how to recognize a potentially dangerous situation and how to avoid becoming a victim. Your school counselor can teach you many strategies on how to react when in an inappropriate or violent situation. You are always correct to remain alert, aware, and disciplined, prepared to respond to any threat or unsafe setting. Make their recommendations and those listed in this book a vital part of your daily crime avoidance and prevention program.

During a Gunfight

How should you react when you hear gunshots? First, you should drop to the ground or sidewalk. I don't care what you are wearing or how muddy the ground is. Drop immediately. Don't run. Flatten out and evaluate the situation. If you are on a sidewalk and there is a curb, try to get behind the curb. Even dumpsters and garbage cans provide some protection. Crawl away from the gunshots if you can't find cover.

Most bullets are flying by at least 18 inches off the ground. The lower you are, the better your chances of surviving. Try to see where the shooting is coming from. Sometimes hysterical people get behind cars only to discover that they are on the wrong side (they can see the shooter), or discover that they have stumbled into the middle of a gang fight.

Get under cover as fast as you can. Cover can be anything that will stop or deflect a bullet. Telephone poles, trees, steel Postal Service mail receptacles, concrete barriers, a car, or a building is suitable. Even a curb or a fire hydrant is better than nothing. Concealment is somewhere to hide, like behind a hedge, but a hedge won't protect you from a bullet.

If you are on foot when the gunfire starts, getting farther away is important. Criminologist J. L. Simmons says that "getting (even) 20 feet away makes you twice as safe as 10 feet away, and 100 feet away is many times safer."

During a Fight

What should you do? The response to this question doesn't require a lot of thought, just common sense. The only response is to leave. The fight may start with fists, but end with weapons. It may also escalate into a gang fight.

> Leave the scene of a fight quickly. It may escalate into a gang fight or weapons may be used.

Now I know that this is difficult. You want to see what happens. Johnny, the bully, is finally getting what he has deserved for years and you want to see every punch. This is not a good decision, however. Your best safety advice is to leave.

Let's say that the bully is being thoroughly defeated by a kid once considered a coward. The bully thought he was a weakling and a wimp. The wimp is a vigilante today, and he's gained 30 pounds this year, so he's decided he isn't going to be pushed around any more. He knocks the bully down with a strong left hook. You laugh and are really amused; after all, this clown has abused you too. Then the bully opens his eyes and looks up at your face, just as you chuckle. It doesn't take a genius to realize that when the bully recuperates, you are going to be his next victim. Don't give the bully another good reason to put you at the top of his persecution list. Leave.

Bomb Scares

Bomb threats are another reality in today's school. Usually the threat is a vicious prank. Somebody is bored or they want the school evacuated because they are not prepared for today's test. Even in revolutionary lands, 99 percent of all bomb threats are hoaxes. On any given day when there is a bomb threat, the chances are that this is not a real danger.

Schools, however, must react to threats of this type to ensure the safety of every student. Usually this includes a thorough search of the school property by authorities. Sometimes firefighters, police officers, bomb dogs, and EMTs (emergency medical technicians) come to search as well. The best thing that you can do is to follow the directions of your teachers and school administrators.

Sometimes the bomb threats are real. Several bombs were detonated at Columbine High in Colorado during the deadly attack in 1999. One of them went off the night after the attack. Bomb squads defused several other active bombs. One of these had been placed with bags of nails, broken glass, and an egg timer around a 20-pound propane tank. Had these bombs detonated, more students would have been maimed or killed.

If there really is a bomb, what can you do to increase the likelihood of survival? Again, the best thing that you can do is to follow the directions of school authorities. If they want to evacuate, then do so in an orderly fashion. Don't rush out. But, don't dawdle, either. Your risk is increased whenever you speed ahead or drag behind those evacuating the area.

If I were afraid there was a bomb, I would prefer to be in the center of a crowd of other students. Most bomb victims are not hurt by the explosion itself. They are injured by glass and shrapnel. In a bomb threat, the worst place you can stand is adjacent to a window. If there is no alternative, then stand with your back to the window. If there are any curtains , shades, or blinds, use them.

Any cover is better than none because the glass shards may blind you if you are looking toward an explosion when the windows disintegrate. The hallways are safer than the classrooms, just as in a tornado drill. The building has its strongest reinforcements there.

References

1. *Violent schools—safe schools: The safe school study report to the Congress.* 1978. Washington, D.C.: Superintendent of Documents, 92.
2. Cuervo, A. G., J. Lees, and R. Racey. 1984. *Toward better and safer schools.* Alexandria, VA: National School Boards Association, 12.
3. *CCHR Working Group on School Violence/Discipline.* 1984. Memorandum for the cabinet council on human resources concerning disorder in our public schools. Rockville, MD: National Institute of Justice, National Criminal Justice Reference Service, 20–21.

10

Teenage Rape and Sexual Assault Avoidance

Elizabeth is the editor of the school yearbook. She frequently stays after school to work with Mrs. Jones, the English teacher responsible for this annual publication. Late Tuesday afternoon, Elizabeth walked down the hall to use the restroom. As she was leaving, a large boy came in, blocking her way. He was gross, nasty, and rude. He told Elizabeth that he was going to have sex with her, but he used four-letter words. She wanted to run, but this big, crude monster was blocking her way.

Elizabeth's heart was in her throat because she was so scared. She didn't say a word, but pretended compliance. Nodding, she turned and walked back toward the stalls. The ruse worked as the intended rapist vacated his vigil before the door. She saw her chance and jerking past him, she ran. She almost made it, too, but he grabbed her from behind. Immediately he grabbed her breast with his left hand and ran his hand down into her pants with his right.

Even though it was unlikely that anyone would hear, Elizabeth began her high-intensity power yell. From deep inside her stomach and lungs, she turned the gift of sound loose in a very resourceful way. As the decibels kicked in, she also stomped her assailant's instep.

Glad that she had worn cowboy boots instead of softer rubber sneakers that day, she let him have it. As she stomped, he loosened his grasp with his right hand. Twisting just a little, she back-handed his crotch, really hard, again and again and again. Like a drummer, she let her fist run a staccato beat.

When he screamed and released her, she ran out the door and down the hall to the school security resource officer. Her attacker was still in the ladies room, sobbing in pain, when the school security officer arrested him. Three days later, when Elizabeth saw him for the preliminary hearing at the county court house, he could barely walk.

Elizabeth is a successful victim. Yes, she has nightmares about this character and he touched her in awful ways, but she wasn't raped, and she really has stronger self-esteem than ever before. In fact, her classmates gave her a nickname. She is now called "Tuffe," a personal descriptor for "tough enough."

Rape Can Happen to Anyone

The United States has the world's highest rape rate of the countries that publish rape statistics.[1] American women are several hundred times more likely to be raped than are women in other countries.[2] Our rape rate is 4 times higher than that of Germany, 13 times higher than that of England, and 20 times higher than that of Japan.[3]

In fact, statisticians indicate that about one out of every four girls will be raped (or a serious attempt to rape will be made) by the time she reaches 21. *A disproportionate percentage of rape victims are attacked before their 15th birthday,* raped before they can legally drive. In fact, 29 percent of all reported rapes occur before a girl's 11th birthday and 32 percent occur between the 11th and 17th year, thus 61 percent of all reported rapes occur before the 17th birthday.[4]

Over 40 percent of all rapes occur in the girl's home,[5] the one location she should feel safe. When you talk about rape, you should talk about avoidance, deterrence, and prevention. By the time a rape attempt is initiated, it may be too late. In fact, rapes are so frightening that only about one third of all victims are strong enough to say, "No."[6] Only about 12 percent of rape victims even try to resist in any way.[7] Only about 12 percent try to run away.[8] Most rape victims are incapacitated by their fear, even to the point that they don't say no and they don't even scream.

The time to avoid rape is *before it happens.* Obey the safety and security rules set by your parents and school. Obeying the school policy manual protects you, sets limitations on the behavior that can occur, and keeps you from having a lifetime of guilt and nightmares.

The first thing to realize is that rape can happen to you. The girls most likely to be raped are the ones who refuse to listen to good advice. They believe rape isn't going to happen to them, so they don't listen. Without this knowledge, they are much more likely to be attacked. They are in denial. "Nice girls aren't raped." "I don't have to worry, my daddy, brother, or boyfriend will look after me." "I'm too young." "I'm too fat." "I'm too skinny." "My chest is flat and I am not attractive." "I have pimples." " My braces are as big as a car bumper." "I'm not pretty enough to be raped." "Athena Erotic over there, the one with the *Playmate Magazine* physique, the big chest and well-rounded hips, is likely to be raped, not me."

However, this is *not* the way rapists pick victims. Rapists pick *naïve* girls who don't think they will be raped. They pick somebody vulnerable and alone. They pick soft targets. They pick girls who are so lax and unaware that they probably can't identity the creep who rapes them. They pick young girls who take unnecessary risks. They don't necessarily pick the girl most likely to become a movie star or a professional model. Date rapists pick girls who believe that they can always talk a boy out of their attack. By refusing to accept rape as a real possibility, most girls do not learn the PINs (preincident indicators).

THREE CATEGORIES OF GIRLS

1. Some girls make things happen.
2. Some girls discover that things are always happening to them.
3. Some girls don't know what is happening. These girls are in the highest risk category.

There are three categories of girls. Some make things happen. They are assertive leaders. The second category includes the weak. Things are always happening to them. They are at risk. It's the third category, however, which is alarming. The girls most at risk are the girls who *don't know what is happening*. They are naïve, indecisive, and weak. From the criminal's point of view, they are *good victims*.

In writing *Safe: Not Sorry*, Tanya Metaksa said:

If women spent as much time actually thinking about taking real precautions as they do in preparing their hair and makeup, they would find that they were ready to defend themselves against almost any kind of violence. And, by being prepared, they might even prevent a violent act.[9]

Prerape Interviewing

Many rapists "interview" their victim. They talk to them before they attack. (Often such interviews occur before assaults, robberies, or even house burglaries as well.) The crooks want to know what they are dealing with, but, in this particular interview, they are contemplating rape. The interview may be about anything or nothing. It will *not* be about sex. This would make most girls feel uncomfortable, especially with a stranger. No, this guy is just trying to discover if you will be a "good" victim.

The rapist is interviewing, trying to determine your awareness level. He may ask for change, a match, or directions. He is looking to see what your boundaries are. He is testing you to see how far he can go. If he senses excessive nervousness, he knows you are on to him. In a public place, leave quickly. In a private place, start running and yelling.

Frequently, the rapist will touch the girl in the interview. He will probably touch your arm or shoulder first, or if you both are sitting, your knee. The touch won't be extraordinarily suggestive at first, but it sets a stage for more intimate touching. Stop the touching immediately, establish your boundaries, and tell him to leave. This really establishes "your space." If he doesn't leave, then you should.

Some interviews are "silent." Nothing is said. The guy watches you, looking for weakness, a heavy load, inattention, or a lack of awareness. Then he jumps you. If you are inattentive, you will never even see him watching you nor do you witness his approach.

Prerape Tests

Sometimes creeps will see how far they can intrude into your space. They see if they can violate your "safety circle." Often they will purposefully brush up against you to see how you will react. Most girls just move over, preferring not to make a scene. When a guy brushes up against your breasts or your hips, however, you *should* make a scene. While it is possible that this touching could have been "accidental," especially in a crowd, a bus, or a subway, in all likelihood, it was purposeful.

Think about it. Did anyone, ever, brush up against your breasts, stroke your buttocks, or touch your thighs before you started to develop into womanhood? Probably not. Why do you suddenly feel uncomfortable about guys touching you? You feel uncomfortable because it's not right and because it's probably not accidental.

Don't let this character think you are a docile pushover. Don't let him "violate" your space and, most especially, don't let him touch you. Respond in a loud voice. "Back off! Get away! Don't you touch me again." Don't move out of your space. Make *him* move, by the sheer power of your words, your personality, and your assertiveness. After all, you were there first.

I know that you don't think that "nice" girls should be rude, but this is an exception. Don't be afraid to be rude. Your personal safety is much more important than his feelings. Remember, too, that most rapists want a victim, not a fight.

By being assertive and standing up for your rights, you are decreasing the likelihood that you will become a rape victim. However, in demanding your rights, don't be mean spirited. He will respect you for being assertive, but if you get mad and call him profane names or speak to him in a derogatory manner, you may actually increase your chances for a future assault or rape.

By the same token, if you allow him to get too close, you are sending another silent message. "I'll be a good victim." If you merely move away, or worse yet, remain in that location, he'll cut you off later, isolate you, and rape you. He has already learned that you will be safe to attack.

Many girls choose to retreat and suffer in silence, rather than making a scene. They probably believe that this is the most "ladylike" option. Unfortunately this reaction is a serious blunder. Silence can even be deadly when you are looking at a predator. When you retreated, you showed him in a very clear way that he could successfully encroach upon your space and that you will be compliant. Don't make the compliance mistake. You need to be assertive, but remember not to be aggressive. You don't want to infuriate this creep so badly that he stalks you until he "gets" you.

Good posture is one of the best rape avoidance techniques. Keep your head up and your shoulders back. I'm not saying to exaggerate your posture to get another inch of bust line. I'm merely talking about a positive bearing and good posture, both of which suggest assertiveness. Self-reliant and assertive girls make terrible rape victims.

Rapists want an over-compliant couch potato. Shy, timid, fearful, weak, and young girls are much more likely to be raped. Your bearing, posture, and attitude can decrease the likelihood of rape and all other street crimes. Assertive girls are rarely raped, and then only when they made unacceptable safety choices or are defiant about reasonable rape precautionary procedures.

Assertive girls know what to say. They communicate well. "What part of the word NO are you having difficulty understanding?" They are precise, direct, and appropriate to the situation. They are not afraid of being uncooperative, discourteous, or even rude to a despicable example of humanity.

School is a priority location for a rape as well. The National School Board Association reported that 7 percent of the violent acts committed at school involved rape.[10] In large urban school districts, the rate is 20 percent.[11] While many people are usually at school during normal hours, this is not true either before or after school. Even during school, if a girl can be isolated, she can be raped.

One junior high school student I interviewed told me that she was attracted to a fellow classmate. He already had a girlfriend, but this teen thought she was in love. This fellow talked her into going into an unused school dressing room with him. She thought they would talk, hold hands, and maybe kiss a little. She did want a little romance, but she didn't want sex and she certainly didn't want rape. Had she stayed in public view, she wouldn't have been attacked. She feels very guilty because she was gullible enough to follow his directions.

Pick your spots when you date or even when you arrange a meeting. Rape can happen anywhere, but it is far more likely to happen at certain sites and times. Higher risk locations can be avoided when you do the picking.

Obeying the rules at school can help save you from the tragic consequences of this despicable act. Even with all the vulgar words you hear at school, rape is still the ugliest four-letter word in the entire English language. School grounds, school parking lots, school buildings, and sports bleachers may all camouflage the ever-present attack dangers.

Rape Myths

Your perception of a rapist is probably a myth. More than likely, you think a rapist looks dumb, is probably of another race, has heavy eyebrows, has maniacal facial characteristics, and can overpower any woman. This stereotype is misleading. Most rapists are working-class men or professionals. Many are doctors, preachers, and lawyers. These guys undress you with their eyes before they attack you. When they look at you inappropriately, you're getting an early warning, a preincident indicator.

The truth is that the rapist is normally of above-average intelligence. A large percentage are young, but many rapists are married guys with families. They come from all economic and family backgrounds, occupations, ethnic groups, and cultures.

There is also a *myth of race*. In the United States, only about 20 percent of all rapes reported to the police involve people of a different race.[12] It is noted that 80 percent of all rapists attack girls or women of their own race.[13] This tells us that you should worry more about your boyfriend, neighbor, or the boy sitting beside you in class. *Stereotypes increase your risks because you avoid guys who probably won't hurt you and then you end up taking risks with guys who will.*

Date Rape Prevention

Co-author Chester Quarles and his wife have one daughter and four sons. We had high standards for Kathy and her brothers. When Kathy started dating, we wanted to know the boy and we wanted to know his parents. On every date, he was to come in and meet us. If a boy had honked from our driveway, I would have told him to leave—without Kathy. Some of you readers may believe that this is an archaic practice left over from the dark ages, but, in fact, this practice protects you. Visiting with parents is not only courteous, it is a strong security approach.

I always talked to Kathy's date about where they were going, what they were going to be doing, if any adult chaperones would be at these events, and when they were returning. I always let the boy know that I personally held him accountable for her safety. Kathy always had to be in by 10:30 or 11 p.m. Kathy lived at home even during her college years and these time limits continued until she was married.

We live in a university community, but there isn't any acceptable activity for high-standard young people after the movie theater, the bowling alley, or the skating rink closes. In fact, getting drunk, getting high, or getting pregnant seemed to be the only late-night youth activities I could envision. And, I continue to be aware that automobile fatalities spiral out of control after midnight, usually relating to alcohol abuse, and that the violent crimes of assault, car jacking, rape, and murder increase dramatically during the early hours of the a.m. I believe that 11 p.m. was a good standard three decades ago and it still is.

Date Rape

Date rape is a problem for women of all ages. The criminological literature gives a clear indication of the type of guy who will rape on a date or social occasion. In a Florida survey of young rape victims, approximately 97 percent of them knew their attackers.[14]

THE DATE RAPIST

- Someone the victim knows.
- Does not respect your wishes.
- Makes you feel uncomfortable.
- Talks about sex.
- Attempts to isolate you, get you off alone with him.
- Tries to be romantic, first attempting seduction.
- Starts touching or pawing you when seduction is unsuccessful.
- The intensity of his attack escalates when you say "no" or try to stop him.
- Attack! Rape!

Rapes committed on a date or by someone you know well seldom occur without warning. There are several PINs that will serve as warnings. Acquaintance rapists exhibit several forms of inappropriate behavior. Craig Huber and Don Paul state that the warnings are from the rapist's eyes, his mouth, and his hands.[15]

Taking note of eyes, mouth, and hands can save you a lot of discomfort later. When I mention eyes, I'm not talking about the appreciative look of a boy who thinks you're pretty or who thinks your new outfit is stylish. In most cases, an appreciative look of someone you care about is flattering, especially if this is your favorite somebody or if you are in love. The look I'm talking about is negative, cheap, tawdry, and lewd. The boy undresses you with his eyes, stares at your body, and makes you feel uncomfortable. He should be looking at your eyes, not at your breasts, hips, or thighs.

The mouth itself, what he says, and the motion of his mouth is another PIN. Is his speech demeaning or vulgar? Does he talk about sex in a degrading way? Does he curse and use cheap four-letter words? Does every conversation revert to sex? And, why does he want to talk about sex when you were talking about homework? If his compliments make you feel debased rather than flattered, then you have already keyed in on another warning.

Some date rapists are totally inconsiderate of their date's feelings. Does your date belittle you? Does he act in a dominating or hostile way toward you or other girls? Does he act like he owns you? Is he always negative about girls? Does he treat you in a subservient manner? Is he angry at the world? If he's full of resentment, he won't be a good date anyway. Don't just go along with what your date wants. Don't always be submissive. Don't let him always pick the movie or the restaurant, or the entertainment. You pick it.

If things work out, and you date this fellow for a while, *then* let him choose, but don't ever be a pushover. The real message you need to send him is that you will not be a compliant, nonresisting victim. You *will* tell on him later if he touches you inappropriately, or harms you in any way. Terminate any relationship that is forceful, even if the force is psychological instead of physical. Either way, you should know that you are going to be harmed.

If you begin to feel uncomfortable during a date, listen to your instincts. Call your family or a friend. Use any excuse to get away. If you don't feel safe, refuse to ride home with him. Date rape police files are full of examples where the victim had strong intuitive feelings that something wasn't right, but failed to act on these feelings.[16]

If you are attacked, you can escape, submit, or fight. Decide today what you will do and prepare for this possibility. Authorities generally agree that the sooner a girl defends herself, the more she is likely to avoid rape.

GIRLS WHO AVOID RAPE

- Freak out
- Get really mad
- Have a fit
- Power yell
- Run away
- Escape

Don't be afraid to resist. Girls are often injured in a rape attempt, just as they are injured in resisting, but self-defense and then escape are usually the best responses in a date rape attempt. Girls who avoided rape remember freaking out, getting really angry, going ballistic, screaming, and running; these were the girls who avoided rape.

Every rape avoidance activity is intended to help you escape. Even if you must fight, it is to gain the opportunity to run, not to duke it out with a fool. Some girls do pretty gross things to avoid rape. Tell the hormonally influenced, sex pig that you are menstruating. Stick your finger down your throat to the point of choking. Throw up! Defecate! If Johnny Romeo is pawing you, and won't stop, vomit all over him. Let's see how sexy he thinks you are when he's wiping your puke off his new jacket or when he is smelling body waste on his car seat. He will probably lose his erotic fantasy completely.

Date rapists not only have Roman hands (roaming hands) and Russian (rushing) fingers, they like to touch you a *lot*. All of the touching is not necessarily unacceptable, but if holding *his* hand or hugging *him* makes you feel uncomfortable, you are out with the wrong boy. Listen to your feelings. *If his touch feels terrible, then you are too close. You're in trouble.* Get away from him quickly. Call home and let your folks pick you up. They will be glad to come. Then stay away from him in the future. Don't go out with him again and tell your friends what he is like. He will continue his activities as a sexual predator until he is stopped.

Another PIN is to beware of a boy that other boys don't like. Sometimes people are misjudged, but by and large, there is a reason for most behavior. Just as girls talk to other girls and share their innermost thoughts, so do boys. If the boys feel uncomfortable around Sensual Joe Sleazeball, you should pay attention to this fact as well.

A slob like Sensual Joe is probably telling the boys that he is "making it" with you even when he doesn't have the nerve to attempt a kiss. If you get a bad reputation, deserved or not, you are in another kind of trouble. Other guys may think you are *easy*. Fewer guys will accept "no" for an answer. They "know" you are sexually experienced because of the "facts" Sleazeball told them, so what's the big deal if you do it again with them? Always acting like a lady will counter Sleazeball's claim with most observers.

WHEN THE STORM OF RAPE GETS CLOSER

- His *eyes* devour you.
- His *mouth* is out of control.
- His *hands* roam freely, even when you attempt to restrict his movements.

Except in date rape, many girls think some character jumps out of a nightmare and into their life, totally surprising them. It is called a blitz rape, after the German Nazi bombing of England in World War II; actually it only occurs in a small percentage of all rapes. If he has a knife or gun, you probably shouldn't resist. If he is just using superior strength and weight to his advantage, you may choose to resist.

Watch the Men Watching You

Girls are really at risk. It's like your city or town is a war zone. You never know when the enemy will strike. He chooses when to attack and where to attack. You can only attempt to defend yourself at that time and at that site. The best behavior is to stay out and away from possible rape situations. Avoid excessive risk, creepy boys, and dangerous locations, while paying special attention to the boys or men paying attention to you.

References

1. National Center for Victim of Crime. 1992. *Rape statistics.* Washington, D.C.: NCVC, April 23.
2. Simmons, J. L., and G. McCall. 1992. *76 ways to protect your child from crime.* New York: Henry Holt and Co., 157.
3. National Center for Victim of Crime.
4. National Center for Victim of Crime. 1992. *Rape in America: A report to the nation.* Washington, D.C.: NCVC and the Crime Victim's Research and Treatment Center.
5. National Institute of Law Enforcement and Criminal Justice. 1977. *Forcible rape: Police volume I.* Washington, D.C.: U.S. Government Printing Office, 19.
6. Ibid.
7. Ibid.
8. Ibid.
9. Metaksa, T. K. 1997. *Safe, not sorry.* New York: HarperCollins, xviii.
10. Day, N. 1996. *Violence in schools: Learning in fear.* Springfield, NJ: Enslow Publishers, 58.
11. Ibid.
12. Bower, L. E. 1981. Women as victims: An examination of the results of the L.E.A.A.'s National Crime Survey Program. In *Women and crime in America,* pp. 164–165. New York: McMillan.
13. Ibid.
14. Lang, M. 1993. Date rape: A fear many teens live with. *Tallahassee Democrat,* January 25, 150.
15. Huber, C. and D. Paul. 1993. *Secure from crime,* 2nd ed. Woodland, CA: Path Finder Publications, 110.
16. Simmons and McCall, *76 Ways,* p. 153.

11

WHAT ARE YOU GOING TO DO NOW?

This is an important question. You have read a lot of material. You have been shown how to be safer and more secure. You have been shown the crime avoidance and personal survival approaches of many successful victims. However, the decision on whether you accept these tactics, reject these tactics, or remain complacent is still yours to make.

Certainly I would agree that there are no guarantees that you can always prevent any individual crime. No one can always predict everything, from the weather to a criminal attack, but you can usually predict those "human" things that are likely to happen to you. Which of the possibilities is probable at your school or in your neighborhood? Decide what is likely to happen to you.

Tim Powers and Richard Isaacs, in *The Seven Steps to Personal Safety* (Center for Personal Defense Studies, 1993), wrote about "when/then" exercises. *When* a street assault occurs, *then* I will _____. *When* a robbery attempt occurs, *then* I will _____. *When* a rape attempt occurs, *then* I will _____. Plan ahead. Know how you will respond. Know what you want and need. Some victims may want revenge, so a street-tough gang member may want to fight it out with his assailant. If you are an average teenager, however, you should only use such force as is necessary to escape. Survival is the final exam and the only conclusive measure of success after a criminal attack.

When You Are Attacked

When attacked or when you suspect an attack, you need to evaluate the situation. Then you need to respond reasonably—not too much, but not too little, either. The best approaches always center around deterring or avoiding your crime. Reactionary steps are responses to an attack that has already begun.

As we interviewed older children and teenagers all over the United States, we found that many have lost faith in the American dream. They feel threatened, isolated, and alone. Many believe the situation is hopeless because teen violence is escalating and because they are afraid. As a police and security professional and as a professional counselor, this point of view really disturbs us.

We have seen communities, public housing developments, schools, and individuals become safe and secure even though they had experienced extraordinarily high crime rates in the past. For the past 20 years, Chester Quarles has helped build security and safety out of chaos and peace out of anarchy. He has even applied most of these crime prevention methods in foreign countries, where American missionaries and humanitarian and aid workers were being targeted for robbery, rape, kidnapping, bombing, and murder.

Tammy Quarles worked in a neighborhood school where violence was a normal part of the culture and violence counseling an expected part of professional service. We know these methods work, but we also have become aware of the fact that very few teenagers understand crime prevention or crime deterrence. They need to understand what a "security consciousness" is all about.

Most teenagers aren't concerned with security, not until they become a crime victim. Then it is too late. The trauma, psychological fear, and personal injuries are harmful in many ways beyond the stress of the crime itself. Those most injured are the naïve victims who thought that "it won't happen to me."

Accept the Probability of Crime

The first step toward personal safety and security is to accept the fact, even the probability, that you will become a victim before your 19th birthday. The next step is to plan to avoid that probability and to train yourself in avoidance techniques. To accomplish this objective, you *must accept responsibility for your own security*. You can't delegate it to anyone else. Mom or dad will serve as your loving guardians, but, in many cases, you may be the most *streetwise* member of your family.

With information and misinformation overwhelming the average student, it is little wonder that parents, teenagers, and younger children just don't know what to do. The multiplicity of choices is confusing. Mr. Security (Issy Boim) wrote, "We're drowning in information and starving for knowledge."[1] With *Staying Safe at School* preparation, you don't have to be confused. Discuss your security choices, decisions, and options with your parents and other responsible adults.

American teenagers are overwhelmed with crime information. You read and hear about so many reports that you become conditioned to it. It is kind of like cancer, almost every family has some. You expect crime, especially in poor neighborhoods, but somewhere in the recesses of your mind, you expect it to happen somewhere else, to someone else in another neighborhood, perhaps in another town. In spite of all the statistical data, you think that you will not be victimized.

The most important thing you can to do to avoid crime is to *learn to be aware*. Be aware of your surroundings. Be aware of the school. Be aware of the neighborhood. Be aware of who is around you, especially those approaching *your circle of safety*. Let crime prevention and crime avoidance become your best and strongest habit.

Concentrating on your problems, daydreaming, or philosophical contemplation can be dangerous. A vigilant and observant attitude should become a way of life. Police officers, security agents, and soldiers reflect this attitude; they have to or they will not survive. By walking with your shoulders squared and with an erect bearing, you are lowering the chance that you will become a crime victim. By always looking, *seeing* what you observe, and interpreting your observations correctly, you can avoid victimization.

Listen to Your Feelings

You also should listen to your feelings. Intuition is your best friend. If you are suddenly frightened, then *listen carefully to your feelings*. Do something about your fear, however. Don't suffer in silence. Leave! Get out of there. Don't ignore these feelings. Don't talk yourself out of them. Do not let reason or logic influence your decision. Leave!

Become a hard target, not a soft, easy target. Target hardening is a practical philosophy that decreases crime against you. It keeps your crime from occurring. Your crime is deterred when prevention and avoidance methods are accepted as a way of life. Your crime is avoided when you see the PINs (preincident indicators) and leave in time.

Your crime is avoided when you make a criminal work harder, make it more difficult for him to succeed, make access to you more difficult, and his escape more problematic. Any of these factors reduces his ability to succeed or at least shakes his confidence level about successfully targeting you, getting away, and avoiding arrest. Decreasing *his* security increases *yours*. Increasing *his* risk, lowers *yours*. Remember a crook, even a teenage crook, is just another business person wanting to get a quick return for little risk. Take away the quick return or increase the risk, and the criminal activity is deterred.

Keep your mind on what you are doing and where you are going. Watch, look, and listen. Watch for the "whos." The who might be a Gangster Disciple, a bully, a drug pusher, a MICA (mentally incompetent, chemically addicted), or a creep. Remember that the "whos" are the ones who commit crime. Watch for troublesome people. Avoid walking near them. Change directions or walk across the street.

If people are arguing, mind your own business. If someone is having sex in a car parked at the curb where you are walking, don't get caught peeking. If there is a fight, leave as quickly as you can. Always consider alternatives for leaving quickly. Perhaps you could jump in an available taxi and pay the driver to take you away quickly. Perhaps you could step onto the bus that is stopped at the corner. Perhaps you should run down the sidewalk entrance toward the subway station and leave the threat behind you. If you aren't aware, however, you will miss all of the opportunities for avoiding this threat.

Hold your head up. Keep a strong bearing and good posture. Look around, observe, interpret what you see in terms of the daily crime news. Don't walk with your hands in your pocket and don't carry things in your hands if you can avoid it. That's why you have a backpack. You can't defend yourself if you are encumbered with your books and your lunch. If you see something that bothers you, leave. If you must, run! If your backpack slows you down, toss it. Run as fast as you can until you get somewhere safe, such as a police or a fire station. At night, your run might be from total darkness into a well-lighted area.

Accept the Responsibility

Accepting the responsibility for your own safety is an appropriate decision. You know that crime can occur at any time. It can occur anywhere. However, it is more likely to occur at certain locations and at specific times. Having done your homework and having developed your security program is a major step. You must be able to analyze your own risk.

Accepting responsibility for your own safety takes the four Cs (character, confidence, courage, and common sense). Responsible, law-abiding teenagers are careful about safety and security issues. They accept responsibility for what they do and for what they don't, but should.

Accepting the responsibility feels good too. You don't have to worry about how the teacher, the coach, the principal, the business owner, the police officer, or other possible guardians are going to help. While you will use these resources where you find them, holding yourself responsible and accountable is a healthy attitude and encompasses a healthy state of mind.

Mr. Security (Issy Boim) says: Responsibility + preparation = The ability to meet unexpected challenges.

After you have accepted responsibility, the next step is preparing for these possibilities or probabilities, then you will be ready for any security challenge. You will *be prepared*, just like the Boy Scout motto requires. You will be ready to face a criminal attack with more confidence than ever before. You will be prepared to react to a criminal attack.

Being Prepared Has Tremendous Benefits

"YOUR CRIMINAL" DOES HAVE AN ADVANTAGE

- He knows when he will attack.
- He knows where he will attack.
- He takes the initiative.
- He has the element of surprise.
- He acts.
- You must react and respond.

By being prepared and by being aware, and by being ready, you can decrease the advantages every criminal has. If you stay aware and keep all of the security "rules," you will make it difficult for a criminal to corner you, cut you off, or isolate you. If "Crazy Joe" has been stalking you, he already knows your routines and he uses your habits to predict your next move.

By quickly changing the routine when you recognize that you are under surveillance, he will expose himself as your intended assailant. Doing this at a critical moment is decisive and serves to cut off the attack. You disorient your attacker. His predictions about your behavior were invalid. You escape as he hesitates.

Altering your routine suddenly is a threat to your criminal. It reduces his confidence in his ability to complete the crime. By altering your route, or the time you walk to school, you make yourself more difficult to target and you complicate the method of attack. He has already planned his attack; now you are doing something he hasn't predicted and it bothers him. Now he is more at risk. In all probability, he will break off the planned attack and target someone else who is totally unaware of her surroundings or of his surveillance.

You Can Impact Crime

You can impact the crime intended for you, your school, and your neighborhood. You can influence criminals, and you can influence the juvenile delinquents who are now in your age range. Let's keep them out of our schools, out of our communities, and out of our lives. Let's create an environment where their crime is unsuccessful; where they either adjust to a noncrime lifestyle or leave.

Crime, in and of itself, destroys faith in our school, our society, and our government. Crime destroys our faith in each other and creates a mistrust that is harmful to all relationships. Criminals threaten and intimidate us. They reduce the quality of our lives. Let's always recognize the criminals, the thugs, the gangsters for what they are in order that we can defeat them. If we cannot succeed in our own crime prevention program, we must always help the police and justice authorities remove these offenders from society, placing them in the reformatories and prisons where they belong.

Remember too, that in our confrontation society, the proverb, "A soft answer turneth away wrath,"[2] is an appropriate strategy. Sometimes an apology can extricate you from being a victim. Saying, "I'm sorry that I offended you; please forgive me," is not demeaning, even when you have done nothing wrong or when the other person is rude, aggressive, or violent.

References

1. Boim, I. 1997. *Fighting terrorism: The security connection for family protection.* Saline, MI: Safe Flyer Joint Venture Partners, 10.
2. Proverbs 15:1.

Index

A

Absenteeism, 79, *see also* Skipping school
Acceptance, crime risks, 34
Access control, 14
Accessibility, 62
Accessories, *see also* Attracting attention; Clothing
  gangs, 81
  risk reduction, 82–83
  risk removal, 33
  vs. suitability as victim, 47
  winners, 92
Action list, avoiding troublemakers, 82–83
Addy, Bobby, 16
African-American males, 3, 5
Age, risk factor, 4, 5, *xiii–xiv*
Aggression, frowning upon, *ix*
Aid, lending
  "invitation" distraction, 17–18
  in restrooms, 67
  safety, 64
  Sara's example, 44
Air horns, 58, *see also* Boat horns

Alarms
  everyday security decisions, 55–56
  instead of spray, 58
Alcohol, *see also* MICAs (Mentally Incompetent, Chemically Addicted persons); Vulnerability
  substance abusers, 84–85
  vulnerability, 60, 61
Alertness, *see also* Awareness
  crime prevention, 9–10
  personal security program, 46–47
  victim profile, 16
Alleys
  crime reduction, 11
  partnerships, 65
  walking on sidewalks, 62
Alternatives
  routes, 43
  traveling safely, 59, 62–65
Aluminum knuckles, 80
American children *vs.* Northern Ireland, 3
American dream, lost faith, 114

American soldiers, *xiv*

Angry material, students, 27–28

Anonymity
  crime-prevention tactic, 51–52
  weapon carriers, 40–41

A Parent's Guide to Cyberbullying and Cyberthreats, 77

Apology, 119

Appeasement money, 97

Art, *see* Graffiti and symbols

"A soft answer turneth away wrath," 119

Assault, stages of crime, 18

Assertiveness, 105–106

Attaché, 55–56

Attracting attention, *see also* Accessories; Clothing
  everyday security decisions, 51–52
  prerape tests, 104–105
  robbers, 97

Avoidance, *see also* Prevention
  conflict, *xvii*
  crime prevention, 15–16
  less likelihood of attack, *xvii*

Avoidance, sexual assault and rape
  avoiding rape, 110
  awareness of being watched, 111–112
  categories of girls, 103
  date rape, 107–111
  date rapist, 108
  fundamentals, 101–102
  girls who avoid rape, 110
  myths, 107
  prerape interviewing, 104
  prerape tests, 104–106
  prevention, date rape, 107–108
  recognition, getting out of control, 111
  statistics, 102–103

Awareness, *see also* Feelings; Watch, look, and listen
  of being watched, 111–112
  crime prevention, 9–10
  prerape interviewing, 104
  traveling safely, 62–65
  victim profile, 16
  way of life, 115

B

Backpacks, *see also* Purses
  risk reduction, 31
  tossing when running, 116
  what to leave behind, 55

Badges, visitors, 14

Barking dogs, 45

Battery, vehicles, 73

Bearing, *see* Posture

Biblical passage, 119

Bicycles, 73

Bigsville High School, 49

Billy (little brother example), 9

Billy the Bully example, 40–41, 87

Blackjacks, 80

Blind spots, sidewalks, 62

Boat horns, 56, *see also* Air horns

Bobby (big brother example), 9

Boim, Issy, 115, 117

Bomb scares, 99–100

Books, leaving at home, 54

Box cutters, 80

Boys, upbringing influence, *ix*

Boy Scout motto, 117

Brands, 83

Brass knuckles, 80

Brief cases, 55

Bright clothing, 51, 52, *see also* Clothing

Brown, Brookes, 39

Buddy system, 11, *see also*
  Partnerships; Students,
  joining others
Bullies
 avoiding troublemakers, 76–79
 as label, *ix*
 poor parental advice, 6
 preferred targets, 47
 risk transference, 36
Bus travel, 68–69

C

Cabs, *see* Taxi services
Cafeteria, vigilance, 48
Camouflage, administrative
  reactions, 84
Campus Pride campaigns, 83
Candles, 86
Carefulness, 44
Cars, *see* Vehicles
Cash
 hard target, 38
 protection money, 81
 risk spreading, 33
 safety, 64
 soft targets, 36–37
 winners, 92
Categories of girls, 103
CCTV, *see* Closed circuit television
  (CCTV)
Cellular telephones
 communication system weapon,
  56–57
 taxi rides, 70
 when driving, 71
Cemeteries, 86
CGG (Covenant Garden Gang),
  80
Changes
 circumstances, *xvii*
 routines, 118

Character, 117
Charles and Katie (example), 59
Chat rooms, cyberbullies, 77
Chemical addictions, *see* MICAs
  (Mentally Incompetent,
  Chemically Addicted
  persons)
Chemical irritants, 80, *see also*
  Pepper spray
Children's Defense Fund, 3
Cindy (example), 39
Circle of safety, 65, 104–105,
  115
Circumstances, changing, *xvii*
Cliques, 78
Closed circuit television (CCTV),
  41
Clothing, *see also* Accessories;
  Attracting attention
 crime reduction, 10, 11
 everyday security decisions, 50
 gangs, 82
 Middle Eastern women, 52
 risk reduction, 31, 82
 risk removal, 33
 taking off as sign of trust, 96
 vs. suitability as victim, 47
 winners, 92
Cocaine use, 85
Cock-Roach Garden Gang, 92
Collins, Patrick, 45
Colorado, *see* Columbine High
  School
Colors, gang, 83
Columbine High School, 39, 99
Combs, 66
Comfort zone, 64–65
Common sense, 117
Communication systems, 56–57, *see*
  also Cellular telephones
Confidence (displaying), 117
Confidence (lack of), 17, 47

Conflict
  avoidance, less likelihood of
    attack, *xvii*
  resolution skills, 88
Confrontation, stages of crime, 18
Confusion, 60, *see also* Vulnerability
Consideration, lack of, 109
Contemplation, danger of, 115
Context, 25–26
Counselors, *see* School authority
    figures
Countermeasures
  running and power yell, 60
  target hardening, 48
Courage, 117, *xviii*
Covenant Garden Gang (CGG), 80
CPTED, *see* Crime Prevention
    though Environmental
    Design (CPTED)
Crack heads, 85, *ix*
Creeps, as label, *ix*
Crime avoidance partnerships
  traveling safely, 65–66
Crime elements, 13–15
Crime prevention
  alert and awareness, 9–10
  avoidance, 15–16
  deterrence, 15–16
  elements to every crime, 13–15
  fundamentals, 9
  ingredients of crime, 10
  lowering risk, 14
  opportunity model, 12
  reduction of crime, 10–12
  stages of crime, 17–18
  traits of victims, 17
  understanding how criminals
    work, 11
  victim profile, 16–17
Crime Prevention though
    Environmental Design
    (CPTED), 15

Crimes committed by juveniles, 4
Crime Stopper programs, 40
Crimes zones, 23–24
Criminals
  element of crime, 14
  understanding how they work,
    11
*Crisis Management: Planning for the
    Inevitable,* 25
Crying, 96
Cyberbullies, 77

D

Dangerous places
  at school, *xvii*
  school as most, 5–6
Dangerous students, 87
Dark alleys, *see* Alleys
Date rape
  fundamentals, 108–111
  picking own spots to avoid, 106
  prevention, 107–108
Date rapist, 108
David and Suzy, 87–88
*Davis v. Monroe County Board of
    Education,* 9
Daydreaming, danger of, 115
Dead battery, vehicles, 73
DeBecker, Gavin, 25–26, 63
Decapitated teenagers, 86
Deception, crime reduction, 11–12
Decisions, everyday security
  attracting attention, 51–52
  clothing, 50
  communication systems, 56–57
  fundamentals, 49
  handbags, 55
  pepper spray, 57–58
  possessions, 53–55
  power yell, 56
  school uniforms, 50–51

street crime alarms, 55–56
walking, 53
weapons, 57–58
Delegating security inappropriately, 44–45, *see also* Safety
Denial
administrative reactions, 84
important *vs.* irrelevant information, 26
seeing reality of world, 11–12
Depression
bullying, 78
staring at floor, 47
Deterrence, 15–16
Difference, making, 7
Directions, asking for, 44
Discourteous behavior, permission, *ix*
Disobeying parents, 35
Disrespected (dissed), 2, 93
Distance science/study, 64
Distractions/being distracted
lack of alertness, 47
Sara's example, 44
victim traits, 17
vulnerability, 60
Dogs, 45
Dominic example, 50
Dopers, as label, *ix*
Downplaying, administrative reactions, 84
Dressing, *see* Clothing
Drivers, sitting close to, 69
Driving, traveling safely, 70–73
Dropping out of school, 2, 76
Drug-free schools, 85
Drugs, *see also* MICAs (Mentally Incompetent, Chemically Addicted persons); Vulnerability
substance abusers, 84–85
vulnerability, 60

Dumpsters, 62, 65
Dysfunctional homes, 82

E

Economically stuck, 24
Educational atmosphere, 5–6
Electronic gadgets, 53–55, *see also* Accessories; Technology
Elements to every crime, 13–15
Elizabeth (example), 101–102
E-mail, cyberbullies, 77
Entrapment, 41
Everyday security decisions
attracting attention, 51–52
clothing, 50
communication systems, 56–57
fundamentals, 49
handbags, 55
pepper spray, 57–58
possessions, 53–55
power yell, 56
school uniforms, 50–51
street crime alarms, 55–56
walking, 53
weapons, 57–58
Exclusion from groups, 77, 78
Exercises, "when/then," 113
Eye contact
friendliness, 39
safety, 64
using inappropriately, 107, 109

F

Facial expressions, 64
Facts, *see* Statistics
False rumors, 28
Familiar routes, 61–62
Family economics, 24
Fatigue, 60, 61

Fear
    denial of, *x*
    facing, *xviii*
    Lane family example, 1–2
    making a difference, 7
    most dangerous place, 5–6
    national survey, 2–4
    risk assessment, 26
    statistics, 4–5
    staying home from school, 2
Federal Office of Juvenile Justice
        Delinquency Prevention
        Research, 84
Feelings, *see also* Awareness; Watch,
        look, and listen
    interpreting surroundings, 46
    "left out" out of group, 77, 78
    listening to, 12, 109
Fights, successful victims, 98–99
Figure, displaying by walking, 53
Fingers, rushing, 110
Fink, Steven, 25
Firearms, *see* Guns, gunfights, and
        gunfire
"Flash roll" of cash, 97
Flat tires, 73
Forgiveness, asking, 119
Freshman students, 5, 79
Friendliness
    in hallways, 46–47
    less likelihood of attack, *xvii*
    passersby, safety, 64
    personal security program, 47
    risk reduction, 38–41, 82
Frozen fright, 66

G

Gadgets, 53–55, *see also* Technology
Gang members
    arguments with, 80–84
    avoiding troublemakers, 80–84

    colors, 83
    information about an initiation,
        27
    risk transference, 36
Gangsters, as label, *ix*
Gas stations
    filling vehicle gas tanks, 70
    restrooms, 67
Getting out of control, recognition,
        111
*The Gift of Fear: Survival Signals
        That Protect Us from
        Violence,* 25, 63
Gift of observation, 46, *see also*
        Alertness
Girls
    categories, 103
    politeness, 63, 105–106, *ix*
    purses, 65, 67
    who avoid rape, 110
Girls Scout Research Institute,
        78
Gossip, 77, 78
Grade point average, 79
Graffiti and symbols, 83–84, 86
Greeting individuals, 46–47, *see also*
        Friendliness
Groups
    exclusion from, 77, 78
    group paralysis, 66
    traveling safely, 11
Guardians, 16, 68
Guest entrance location, 14
Guns, gunfights, and gunfire
    African-American males, 5
    everyday security decisions,
        57–58
    preschooler deaths, *xiii–xiv*
    shootings listing, *xiv–xvi*
    statistics, *xiii–xiv*
    successful victims, 97–98
Gym, vigilance, 48

H

Hair styles, 83
Hallucinogenic chemicals (THC
    levels), 84–85
Hallways
    friendliness *vs.* staring, 46
    as hot spots, 23
    intersecting, 14
    vigilance, 47
    walking in, 53
Handbags, 55, *see also* Purses
Hands
    in restrooms, 67
    roaming, 110
Hard targets, 37–38, 46, 115, *see
    also* Target hardening
Harris, Eric David, 3, 39
Harris Interactive, Inc., 78
Headsets, 47
Heavy load, prerape interviewing,
    104
Helmet, biking, 73
Helping someone, *see* Lending
    aid
Hiding places, staying away from,
    63
High, Brenda, 76
High heels, 53, *see also* Shoes
Home
    in dangerous location, 24
    as dangerous place, 32
    dogs barking, 45
    dysfunctional, 82
    skipping school, 36, 76
Homicide, *see* Murder
Hoover, J. Edgar, 93
Horns, attracting attention with,
    56, 71
Hot spots, 23–24
Huber, Craig, 109
Human sacrifice, 86

I

Identification of troublemakers
    action list, 82–83
    bullies, 76–79
    drug-free schools, 85
    fundamentals, 75
    gang graffiti and symbols, 83–84
    gang members, 80–84
    identifying, 75–89
    list of types, 79
    most dangerous students, 87
    ritualistic groups, 85–87
    safe schools, 85
    substance abusers, 84–85
    tardy students, 79
    truants, 79
    vigilantes, 87–89
    weapon carriers, 79–80
Ignorance, 32
Immobilization, 62, *see also* Moving
Inattention, 60, 104, *see also*
    Distractions/being
    distracted
Inconsideration, 109
Indecision, rape, 103
Indicators, increased risks, 24–26,
    see also Pre-incident
    indictors (PIN)
Influence
    crime reduction, 10
    risks, 34–35
    student government, 15
Information, *see also* Risk
    assessment
    conflicting, 31
    rating system, 28–29
    vs. knowledge, 115
Ingredients of crime, 10
Initiations into gangs, 27
Insecurity, victim characteristic, 47
Instant messaging, cyberbullies, 77

Interpreting surroundings, 46
Intersections, roadways, 71
Interviewing, prerape, 104
Intimidation, victim traits, 17
Intuition, *see* Feelings
Invitation, stages of crime, 17–18
iPods, 53, *see also* Accessories;
    Technology
Isaacs, Richard, 64, 113
Isolation, 62

J

Jack example, 50
Jennie (example), 43
Jerry, 21
Jewelry, *see* Accessories
Jim and Jodie example, 49
Jimmy (example), 92
Jodie and Jim example, 49
Johnny and Robert (example), 65
Johnny (example), 36–37, 87–88, 98
Joining other students
    risk reduction, 35–36
    safety, 63
    vigilance, 48
Jones, Mrs. (example), 101
Jones, Thelma, 16
"Juice," 82
Junior high school, dangerous, 5
Juveniles, crimes committed by, 4

K

Katie and Charles (example), 59
Kinesics, 64–65
Klebold, Dylan, 3
Knives, 57–58
Knowledge *vs.* information, 115

L

Ladylike behavior, 105, 111, *see also*
    Politeness

Lane, Jimbo and Katie, 2
Lane family example, 1–2
Lanes, roadways, 70
Law violations, 13
"Left out" feeling, 77, 78
Lending aid, *see also* Politeness
    "invitation" distraction, 17–18
    in restrooms, 67
    safety, 64
    Sara's example, 44
Lifestyle, security as part of, 32
Lighted areas, safety, 64, 72
Listening to feelings/gut, *see*
    Feelings
Littleton, Colorado, *see* Columbine
    High School
Living in Trouble Lands, 45–46
Lobotomies, 87
Locks, vehicle, 72
Loners as targets, 47
Loose-fitting slacks, 51
Losers and winners, 91–92
Lost, vulnerability when, 60, 61, 62
Louise example, 50
Lowering risk, crime prevention, 14
Lunchroom, *see* Cafeteria, vigilance

M

Making a difference, 7
Making a scene, 104–106, *see also*
    Attracting attention
Managing risks, 32–35
Maps, 22–23
Marijuana, 84–85
Maverick taxi, 69
Meditation, danger of, 115
Mental alertness, 46, *see also* Alertness
Mental incompetence, *see* MICAs
    (Mentally Incompetent,
    Chemically Addicted
    persons)

Metaksa, Tanya, 103
Methamphetamines, 85
MICAs (Mentally Incompetent,
      Chemically Addicted
      persons)
   easily identified, 76
   increased risk from, 24
   substance abusers, 84–85
   traveling safely, 59, 60
Micro-mini skirts, 51, *see also* Clothing
Middle Eastern women, 52
Middle school, dangerous, 5
Mike (example), 91
Mini skirts, 51, 52, *see also* Clothing
Misinformation, 28
Misplaced concerns, 5
Morale, 5–6
Most dangerous students, 87
Motion science/study, 64
Mountain bikes, 73
Moving
   distraction, then stopping, 17–18
   immobilization, 62
   safety measure, 64
Mr. Security, 115, 117
Murder
   African-American males, 3, 5
   getting in assailant's car, 97
Music, *see also* Accessories;
      Technology
   lack of alertness, 47
   what to leave behind, 53
Myths
   rape and sexual assault
      avoidance, 107
   risk reduction, 31–32
   security delegation, 45

N

Naïve victims, 103, 114
Name tags, 31

National Center for Education, 6
National Institute of Education,
      84, 95
National School Board Association,
      106
National School Safety Center
   home as dangerous place, 32
   lack of safety at public schools, 6
   school most dangerous place, 32
   "wolf packs," 81
National survey, 2–5
Negotiation, 96
Neighborhood Watch program, 16
Newspapers
   pre-incident indictors, 24
   reading, 11–12
   risk assessment program, 22
Nickel Mines, Pennsylvannia, 3
Nodding, friendliness, 39
Noisemakers, 55
Nonstandard lifestyles, 81
Northern Ireland *vs.* American
      children, 3
Norwegian Study, 76
Noticing people, *see* Eye contact;
      Friendliness

O

Obedience
   lack of, tragic results, 35
   school rules, avoiding rape, 106
   victim profile, 16
Observation, gift of, 46, *see also*
      Alertness
Oklahoma city bombing attack, 13
Olweus, Dan, 76
Opportunity, 11, 17
Opportunity model, 12
Ostrich method, 34
Others, *see* Joining other students
Outlaws, as label, *ix*

Outside restrooms, 67
Overby, Mr. (example), 37–38

P

Parents
    alerting, gang problems, 84
    calling, date rape, 110
    inability to relate, 4, 6
    not keeping information from,
        1–2
Parking hints, 71, 72
Partnerships, *see also* Students,
        joining others
    buddy system, 11
    bus and subway travel, 68
    less likelihood of attack, *xvii*
    traveling safely, 65–66
Patriot Act, 13
Paul, Don, 109
People, friendly notice, *see* Eye
        contact; Friendliness
Pepper spray, 57–58, *see also*
        Chemical irritants
Permission to be discourteous, *ix*
Perps/perpetrators, 14
Personal actions
    accepting responsibility, 117
    advantage of criminals, 117
    benefits of preparation, 117–118
    community actions, 113–114
    contacting police after crimes,
        95
    feelings, listening to, 115–116
    fundamentals, 113
    imminent attack, 113–114
    impacting crime, 118–119
    probability acceptance,
        114–115
    risk reduction, 31–32
Personal alarms, 55–56, 58
Personal influence, 7

Personal problems, thinking about,
        60
Personal risk factor, determination,
        21–22
Personal security program
    alertness, 46–47
    carefulness, 44
    delegating security
        inappropriately, 44–45
    friendliness, 47
    fundamentals, 43–44
    personal security, 45–48
    target hardening, 48
    vigilance, 47–48
Perverts, as label, *ix*
Philosophical contemplation,
        danger of, 115
Physical aspects, fear, 2–3
Pickpockets, 65
PIN, *see* Pre-incident indictors
        (PIN)
Pin map, 22, *see also* Maps
Place, element of crime, 14
Pleading, 96
Police officers
    alerting to stalkers, 92
    delegating security to, 44–45
    hot spots, 23
    preschooler deaths, comparison,
        xiv
    satanic cults, 87
    school-age population arrests
        statistics, 4
    serious crime notification, 95
Politeness, *see also* Lending aid
    personal safety priority, 105–106
    upbringing influence, *ix*
    using discretion, 63
Pollyanna, *x*
Portable alarms, 58
Possessions, 53–55, *see also*
        Accessories

Posture, *see also* Walking
  rape avoidance, 105–106
  safety, 64, 116
  victim characteristics, 52
Power, 40–41
Powers, Tim, 64, 113
Power yell
  as countermeasure, 60
  everyday security decisions, 56
  traveling safely, 59
Predictable threat, 60
Prefrontal lobotomies, 87
Pre-incident indictors (PIN)
  date rape, 108–109, 111
  leaving in time, 116
  naïve girls, rape, 103
  risk assessment, 24–26
  using eyes inappropriately, 107,
    109
Preoccupation, 60, *see also*
    Distractions/being
    distracted
Preparation, Boy Scout motto,
    117–118
Prerape interviewing, 104
Prerape tests, 104–106
Preschoolers, *xiv*
Prevention, *see also* Avoidance
  crime methods application, 114
  date rape, 107–108
  lowering risk, 14
  reduction of crime, 10–12
  risk reduction, 35
  road map, 10
  stages of crime, 17–18
  understanding how criminals
    work, 11
Primary resources, 26
Principals, *see* School authority
    figures
Principles, action toward bullying,
    1–2

Problems, concentrating on, 115
Prodrome/prodomal, 25
Profit, gang association, 82
Prostitutes, as label, *ix*
Protection money, 81
Proxemics, 64–65
Psychological vulnerability, 60–61
Purses, *see also* Backpacks; Wallets
  in restrooms, 67
  snatching, 54–55
  when partnering, 65
"Pushed-out" of school, 2, 76
Pushover, not being, 109

Q

Quarles, Chester
  be aware, look, listen, 23
  biographical information, *xi*
  bully experience, 25
  clothing children, 50
  crime prevention methods
    application, 114
  date rape prevention, 107–108
  disobeying parents, 35
  security delegation myth, 45
Quarles, Tammy
  biographical information, *xi–xii*
  date rape prevention, 107–108
  security consciousness, 114
  students being bullied,
    estimation, 76–77
  working relationships, 27
Quick stop restrooms, 67, *see also*
    Self-serve stores

R

Race, myth, 107
Radio
  daily newscast, 11
  pre-incident indictors, 24
  risk assessment program, 22

Random crimes, 32, *xvii*
Rape and sexual assault avoidance
     avoiding rape, 110
     awareness of being watched,
          111–112
     cars, rapists hiding under, 72
     categories of girls, 103
     date rape, 107–111
     date rapist, 108
     fundamentals, 101–102
     getting in car, 97
     girls who avoid rape, 110
     Louise example, 50
     myths, 107
     prerape interviewing, 104
     prerape tests, 104–106
     prevention, date rape, 107–108
     recognition, getting out of
          control, 111
     statistics, 102–103
Rating system, information, 28–29,
     see also Risk assessment
Razors, 80
Reaction time, target hardening,
     48
Receiving information, assessment,
     26–28
Recklessness, victim traits, 17
Recognition, getting out of control,
     111
Recruitment, gangs, 80
Red Lake, Minnesota, 3
Reduction of crime, 10–12
Reincarnation, 86
Reliability index, 28–29
Reliable information, 28
Responsibility
     contacting police after serious
          crime, 95
     personal security, 45, 114
Restrooms
     as hot spots, 23

traveling safely, 66–67
     vigilance, 48
Rhetorical hype, 25–26
Rhonnie (example), 43
Richville High School, 75
Ride sharing, 69
Risk
     heedless, victim traits, 17
     ignoring and/or denying, 34, 44
     lowering, 14
     removal, 33, 36
     spreading, 33, 54
     transference, 34, 36
Risk assessment
     crimes zones, 23–24
     fear, 26
     fundamentals, 21, *xvii*
     hot spots, 23–24
     increased risk indicators, 24–26
     information rating system,
          28–29
     maps, 22–23
     personal risk factor,
          determination, 21–22
     pre-incident indictors, 24–26
     receiving/rating information,
          26–29
     reliability index, 28–29
Risk reduction
     accessories and clothing, 82–83
     friendliness, 38–41, 82
     fundamentals, 31, 35
     hard target, 37–38
     joining other students, 35–36
     lifestyle changes, impact, *xvii*
     managing crime risks, 32–34
     managing personal risks, 34–35
     myths, 31–32
     personal actions, 31–32
     prevention approaches, 35
     soft target, 36–37
     target risk, 36–38

Ritualistic groups, 85–87
Road map, prevention strategy, 10
Robbery, 93–97
Robert and Johnny (example), 65
"Roman" hands, 110
Routes
    crime reduction, 11
    traveling safely, 59, 61–62
Routines, changing, 118
Rudeness, *see also* Politeness
    personal safety priority, 105
    using discretion, 63
Running
    tossing backpack, 116
    traveling safely, 59
"Russian" fingers, 110

S

Sadism, 78
Safe: Not Sorry, 103
Safer alternatives, 63–64
Safe schools, avoiding
        troublemakers, 85
Safety, *see also* Security
    circle of safety, 65, 104, 115
    before courtesy, 63
    distance, 64–65
    increasing, *xviii*
    promoting, 7
Safety, traveling
    alternatives awareness, 62–65
    biking, 73
    bus travel, 68–69
    crime avoidance partnerships,
        65–66
    distance science/study, 64
    driving, 70–73
    familiar routes, 61–62
    fundamentals, 59–60
    motion science/study, 64
    parking hints, 71, 72

power yell, 59
psychological vulnerability,
        60–61
restrooms, 66–67
running, 59
safer alternatives, 63–64
school routes, 59, 61–62
subway travel, 68–69
taxi services, 69–70
vulnerability, 60–61, 62
walking in traffic, 61–62, 64
Safety circle, 65, 104–105
Safety helmet, biking, 73
San Francisco crime study, 66
Sara (example), 43–44
Satanic cults, 85–86
Scenes, making, 104–106, *see also*
        Attracting attention
School authority figures
    alerting, gang problems, 84
    denial, 75, 84
    negligence, 88–89
    reporting weapon carriers,
        40–41
    resisting police response, 95
    responsibilities toward students,
        9
    student paper requirements,
        27–28
Schools
    absenteeism, 36, 76, 79
    avoiding troublemakers, 85
    most dangerous place, 32
    recent shootings, listing,
        xiv–xvi
    routes, traveling safely, 59
    students skipping, 36, 76
    uniforms, 50–51
School yard, vigilance, 48
Scream *vs.* power yell, 56
Secondary resources, 27
Secrecy, 40

Security, *see also* Safety
  complacency, 12
  everyday lifestyle, 32
  inappropriately delegation,
    44–45
Security, everyday decisions
  attracting attention, 51–52
  clothing, 50
  communication systems, 56–57
  fundamentals, 49
  handbags, 55
  pepper spray, 57–58
  possessions, 53–55
  power yell, 56
  school uniforms, 50–51
  street crime alarms, 55–56
  walking, 53
  weapons, 57–58
Security, Mr., 115, 117
Self-reliance, 105–106
Self-serve stores, 70
Sensual Joe Sleazeball (example),
  111
Sensual stroll, 53
September 11, 2001, 13
Serial suicide, 86, *see also* Suicide
Service station restrooms, 67
Servitude, 82
The 7 Steps to Personal Safety, 64, 113
Sexual assault and rape avoidance
  avoiding rape, 110
  awareness of being watched,
    111–112
  categories of girls, 103
  date rape, 107–111
  date rapist, 108
  fundamentals, 101–102
  girls who avoid rape, 110
  myths, 107
  prerape interviewing, 104
  prerape tests, 104–106
  prevention, date rape, 107–108

  recognition, getting out of
    control, 111
  statistics, 102–103
Sexual assault tips, 96
Shirley (example), 92
Shoes, 51, 53
Shootings, listing, *xiv–xvi*, *see
    also* Guns, gunfights, and
    gunfire
Shrubs, 62
Shuffle, gang-type, 81
Shyness, 47, 52, *see also* Posture
Sidewalks
  location on when walking, 61
  at night, 11
  safer in center, 63
Silence, deadly, 105
Simmons, J.L., 98
6 o'clock maneuver, 63
Skintight clothing, 51, 52, *see also*
  Clothing
Skipping school, 36, 76, *see also*
  Absenteeism
Skyjacking, opportunity reduction,
  11
Smiling, friendliness, 39
Smith, Jimmy, 37–38
"Soft answer turneth away wrath,"
  119
Soft targets
  listening to feelings, 115–116
  naïve girls, rape, 103
  risk reduction, 36–37
  victim profile, 17
Soldiers *vs.* preschooler deaths,
  xiv
Sophomore students, 5, 79
Spontaneous threat, 60
Spree killers, 3
Stages of crime, 17–18
Staircases, 23
Stalking, 63, 118

Staring
aggressive behavior, 46
compared to friendliness, 39
at floor, 47
traveling safely, 59
Stationary danger, 17–18, *see also*
Moving
Statistics
murders of youth, *xiii*
national survey, 3, 4–5
rape and sexual assault
avoidance, 102–103
teenage victims, *xvii*
The 7 Steps to Personal Safety, 64
Stereotypes, 107
Stop, look, and listen, *see* Watch,
look, and listen
Stoplights, 71
Stopping, 17–18
Street crime alarms, 55–56
Streetlights, 11
Streets, 62–63
Streetwise persons, 114
Strutting, 81
Student Crime Watch, 15–16
Student Justice and Mediation
System, 16
Student paper requirements, 27–28
Students
buddy system, 11
disliked, as target, 47
joining with others, 35–36, 48,
63
most dangerous, 87
skipping school, 76
Students, joining others
buddy system, 11
bus and subway travel, 68
less likelihood of attack, *xvii*
traveling safely, 65–66
Substance abusers, 84–85, *see also*
specific substance

Subway travel, 68–69
Successful victims
bomb scares, 99–100
description of, 92
fights, 98–99
fundamentals, 91
gunfights, 97–98
losers and winners, 91–92
robbery, 93–97
sexual assault tips, 96
tips, 94, 96
winners and losers, 91–92
Suicide, 78, 86–87
Sunlight, avoid looking into, 62
Surveillance, 17, 118
Survival, as winner, 92
Suspect information, 28
Suzy and David, 87–88
Suzy (example), 36–37, 38
Symbols, *see* Graffiti and
symbols

T

Tardiness, 79
Target hardening, *see also* Hard
targets
cash, 38
criminals overlooking/not
seeing, 46
listening to feelings, 115–116
personal security program, 48
risk reduction, 36
Target risks
bullies, 47
risk reduction, 36–38
Tattoos, 83
Taxi services, 69–70
Teachers, *see* School authority
figures
Tear gas, 57–58
Teasing, 77

Technology
    cyberbullies, 77
    everyday security decisions,
        53–55
    hard target, 37–38
    leaving behind, 54
    risk removal, 33
Teenagers
    crimes against, statistics, *xvii*
    decapitated, 86
    school as greatest risk location, 6
Television
    pre-incident indictors, 24
    risk assessment program, 22
    watching nightly news, 11
Tentativeness, victim traits, 17
Tests
    fear level, 4
    prerape, 104–106
Texting
    cyberbullies, 77
    lack of alertness, 47
THC levels (marijuana), 84–85
*The Gift of Fear: Survival Signals
    That Protect Us from
    Violence,* 25, 63
Then exercises, *see* "When/then"
    exercises
The 7 Steps to Personal Safety, 64, 113
Thieves
    hiding under cars, 72
    as label, *ix*
    risk transference, 36
Threats, immediate, 25
Tickets, 69
Tight clothing, 51, 52
Tips, 94, 96
Tiredness, 61, *see also* Vulnerability
Tires, flat, 73
Tormentors, returning to kill, 78
Toy phones, 71
Traffic, walking in, 61–62, 64

Trapped, 62
Traveling safely
    alternatives awareness, 62–65
    biking, 73
    bus travel, 68–69
    crime avoidance partnerships,
        65–66
    distance science/study, 64
    driving, 70–73
    familiar routes, 61–62
    fundamentals, 59–60
    groups, 11
    hot spots, 24
    motion science/study, 64
    parking hints, 71, 72
    power yell, 59
    psychological vulnerability,
        60–61
    restrooms, 66–67
    running, 59
    safer alternatives, 63–64
    school routes, 59, 61–62
    subway travel, 68–69
    taxi services, 69–70
    vulnerability, 60–61, 62
    walking in traffic, 61–62, 64
Trees, 62
Troublemakers, as label, *ix*
Troublemakers, avoiding
    action list, 82–83
    bullies, 76–79
    drug-free schools, 85
    fundamentals, 75
    gang graffiti and symbols, 83–84
    gang members, 80–84
    identifying, 75–89
    list of types, 79
    most dangerous students, 87
    ritualistic groups, 85–87
    safe schools, 85
    substance abusers, 84–85
    tardy students, 79

truants, 79
vigilantes, 87–89
weapon carriers, 79–80
Truants, 79
Trust, 17, 96
2000 Census, 76

U

UCLA (University of California,
Los Angeles), 79
Uncoordinated victims, 47
Understanding how criminals
work, 11
Uniforms, school, 50–51
Unique clothing styles, 51–52
United States Constitution, 85
University of California, Los
Angeles (UCLA), 79
Unlicensed taxi, 69
Unreliable information, 28–29
Unsure, victim traits, 17
Upbringing influence, *ix*
U.S. Anti-Terrorism Bill, 13
*U.S. News and World Report
Magazine,* 6
U.S. Secret Service

V

Valuables in vehicle, 72
Value standard, *xviii*
Vans, danger, 73
Vehicles
distance between, 71
getting in assailant's, 96
hijacking, 70
Sara's example, 44
vans, danger, 73
warning against approach, 63
washing facilities, 70
won't start, 73

Velcro, 66
Very reliable information, 28
Vicki (example), 31
Victimless crime, 84
Victims
element of crime, 13
profile, 16–17
statistics, *xiii, xvii*
traits of, 17
Victims, successful
bomb scares, 99–100
description of, 92
fights, 98–99
fundamentals, 91
gunfights, 97–98
losers and winners, 91–92
robbery, 93–97
sexual assault tips, 96
tips, 94, 96
winners and losers, 91–92
Video cameras, 14
Vietnam *vs.* youth deaths, *xiv*
Vigilance, 47–48, 115
Vigilantes, 87–89
Violent Schools-Safe Schools, 84
Visitor badges, 14
Volunteer security patrols, 16
Vulnerability
increased, 62
naïve girls, rape, 103
psychological, 60–61
victim profile, 17

W

Walking, *see also* Posture
everyday security decisions,
52, 53
gang strut/shuffle, 81
safety posture, 64, 115
on sidewalks, 61
in traffic, 61–62, 64

Wallets, *see also* Backpacks; Purses
  carrying location, 65
  combs, 66
  throwing, 54
Watch, look, and listen, *see also*
      Awareness; Feelings
  hot spots, 23
  interpretation of seeing/hearing,
    18, 116
Watches, *see* Accessories
Wealth, 47, 50
Weapon carriers, 40, 79–80
Weapons, 57–58

Weapons Watch programs, 40
Web pages, cyberbullies, 77
"When/then" exercises, 113
Whistles, 55, 58
"Whos," watching for, 116
Wilson, James Q., 79
Winners and losers, 91–92
"Wolf packs," 81
Wrong place, wrong time, 92

Z

Z subway (example), 91